logolounge 3

2,000 International Identities by Leading Designers

catharine fishel and bill gardner

ROCKPORT PUBLISHERS
BEVERLY MASSACHUSETTS

First published in the United States of America by
Rockport Publishers, a member of
Quayside Publishing Group
100 Cummings Center
Suite 406-L
Beverly, Massachusetts 01915-6101
Telephone: (978) 282-9590
Fax: (978) 283-2742
www.rockpub.com

Library of Congress Cataloging-in-Publication Data available

ISBN-13: 978-1-59253-510-1
ISBN-10: 1-59253-510-0

10 9 8 7 6 5 4 3 2 1

Design: Gardner Design
Layout & Production: *tabula rasa* graphic design
Cover Image: Gardner Design
LogoLounge Font: Baseline Fonts, Nathan Williams

Printed in China

contents

Collections

introduction

LogoLounge.com and the *LogoLounge* book series have been so overwhelmingly embraced by the design community that at times I almost feel a bit embarrassed. Members of the site and readers of the books have asked time and again about their success. The marriage of the site and its books are complex when you start to consider all they offer and the diverse ways they are used. But I have narrowed the answer down to one word: context.

There's another word that is nearly as critical as context—its near twin, content. Since the site's inception at the end of 2001, LogoLounge.com members have submitted more than 100,000 logos as of 2008. Our thousands of members represent every top-tier identity firm in the world and nearly every nation on the Earth. They also represent the genius of small studios that know how to help their clients thrive as top-tier competitors.

Every day, more logos are uploaded to LogoLounge.com, and as amazing and stimulating as these thousands of logos are, they would be perilously close to useless without context. Imagine your desk heaped with thousands of logos, each on a separate slip of paper and in no particular order. It would be of modest value to anyone. Looking for logos of globes, or birds, or leaves, or for a coffee house, or the letter "E"? You could just start digging and, depending on your stamina, you might eventually find something inspirational. Or, if you really had months to invest, you could start to organize the heap.

This absurd situation is pretty close to what happens when you try to find something specific in the mass of books on your shelves, each with its contents randomly organized. Spontaneity is good, but not when you're under the gun and need very specific reference. This is why the book you're holding is filled with 2,000 logos, meticulously organized to allow you to intuitively find inspiration wherever you look and exactly where you expect it.

To add to the book's value, its 2,000 logos are further organized on a companion website at www.logolounge.com/book3. When you log onto this site, you will be able to use the same search tools that LogoLounge.com members use when searching the logos on the site. You can search the contents the way you want to—by keyword, client, industry, designer, style, or date, and even link to a designer's website or email.

Why go to all this trouble? Because we think your time is important. The *LogoLounge* book series and website put inspiration at your fingertips in an instant so that you can spend more time designing and less time playing librarian for the creative universe.

—Bill Gardner and Cathy Fishel

Emanuela Frigerio
C&G Partner, New York, NY

The Dog House logo, by DDB Dallas

"My favorite design is the The Dog House pet grooming logo. I love its simplicity. It is clear, memorable, and timeless—all the attributes a successful logo should have. Though it unmistakably communicates that this is a pet grooming service, it also suggests a business that is caring and professional. The form is pleasing, and the one-color black solution, while basic, is perfect. I have to admit, it even made me smile, which is a rare quality for a logo, indeed."

Born and educated in the fulcro of Italian fashion and industrial design, Emanuela Frigerio has worked in London, Milan, Tokyo, and New York. Clients have included IBM, Knoll, the Museum of Modern Art, the Library of Congress, U.S. General Services Administration, the Rockefeller Foundation, Harry N. Abrams, Crane & Co., and the McNay Art Museum.

A 15-year principal at Chermayeff & Geismar, Inc., she designed a 352-page monograph called *designing* that covers 45 years of the firm's work. She is currently a principal at C&G Partners together with Steff Geissbuhler, Keith Helmetag, and Jonathan Alger.

Connie Birdsall
Lippincott Mercer,
New York, NY

Central Christian Church logo, by Mindspace
"I chose this logo because it engaged me and pulled me into the design on a couple of levels—initially, the sheer restraint and striking elegance of the forms, and then the beautiful discovery of the characters holding hands when you take that second look. Such a wonderfully simple design solution resonates so strongly on many levels: The cross symbolizes Christianity, the people forms represent the church, and the simple use of color communicates the conflict resolution aspect. You don't even need the words. Then, you just can't get it out of your mind. It's sticky and memorable, more signs of a really effective logo design. When a designer gets the execution of the elements just right from a formal graphic perspective and tells a compelling story, it's a real accomplishment."

The professional experience of Connie Birdsall, who leads the design practice at Lippincott Mercer as creative director and senior partner, encompasses 20 years of creating global corporate and brand identity programs, marketing communications systems, information design, launch and implementation programs, and brand management tools. She has led the creative development of branding programs in Asia, Europe, Latin America, and the United States for clients such as Samsung, Citigroup, IBM, Continental Airlines, and, most recently, the Bank of New York and SK Group in Korea. Birdsall frequently shares her insights and professional experiences with student, design, and business organizations. A member of the National Board of Directors of the American Institute of Graphic Arts (AIGA), Birdsall holds a BFA from the Kansas City Art Institute and an MFA from Cranbrook Academy of Art.

Graham Purnell
Cato Purnell Partners,
Melbourne, Australia

Doglogic logo
by Elephant in the Room

"My choice is Doglogic. It made me laugh. The designer obviously understood the core of what had to be communicated and how to do it with style, intelligence, and humor. A great idea, well executed."

Graham Purnell is partner with Ken Cato in Cato Purnell Partners. Under his creative direction, the firm has acquired new clients in a range of industries both in Australia and overseas. After earning a master of art degree from the Royal College of Arts in London in 1984, Purnell worked as senior designer at Minale Tattersfield. He subsequently worked in Singapore with Batey Advertising as design director.

Purnell's work has appeared in many international design publications, including *D&AD, Graphic,* and *Design Downunder.* His work for Energex, Coles Farmland, Kraft, Nestlé Nescafé, Primelife, Royal Guidedogs Association, Suncorp Metway, and many other clients has earned a number of awards for Cato Purnell Partners.

Miles Newlyn

London, England

Kathy Taylor/Acupuncture & Chinese Herbalist logo, by Kahn Design

"I selected Kathy Taylor/Acupuncture & Chinese Herbalist as my favorite. I liked it because it drew me in and made me feel comfortable with alternative medicine. It could be read a number of ways—I like that—but one that appealed was that of knowledge passed from generation to generation. Hands are notoriously difficult to use in logo design, whilst offering great symbolism. This logo used the element of a hand in a way that circumvented the inherent awkwardness, resolving in a beautifully contained shape. A delicate but potent touch."

Miles Newlyn is a renowned typographer, thinker, and designer. He has worked for the world's top branding agencies to create identities for some of the world's leading businesses. Newlyn applies his talents to custom type design as well as logo design and is known for pushing the boundaries of the corporate sector. He has designed many famous logos, including marks for Honda and Unilever, and is also known for helping clients break out of twentieth-century communications strategies and talk today's language of hyperindividualism. Cult designer David Carson describes him as a "type designer extraordinaire," but Newlyn says he simply "designs for people, not markets."

Thomas Vasquez
Brooklyn, NY

MetaCosmetic logo, by GRAF d'SIGN Creative Boutique

"Extremely attractive, the Meta-Cosmetic logo is curvaceous but not overweight, slender without being too thin. It exudes sexuality, has a timeless personal style, expresses originality of thought, reproduces well, is a bit mysterious, and has a sense of humor. But above all, it is smart—and because of that, beautiful. The main problem: It is only a logo."

Since starting his career in the early 1990s in Dallas, Texas, Thomas Vasquez has shaped the way ideas and voices are expressed for some of the world's best-known brands. He has worked with Ogilvy & Mather's Brand Integration Group, creating solutions for IBM, Miller Brewing Co., and Maxwell House, after which he moved to the production company Cyclops. There he created print design and advertising for Levi's, Jockey International, and Universal Music Group, as well as title design work for RCA, ABC, and NBC. He also led the team responsible for rebranding one of the world's most recognizable icons, Elvis Presley.

After leaving Cyclops in 2004, Vasquez began consulting as a freelance design director to advertising agencies: Ogilvy & Mather, BBDO, J. Walter Thompson, DDB, and Berlin-Cameron. He also freelances as an art director for the Sunday edition of the *New York Times.* Most recently, he was chosen by Deutsche Bank to participate in a three-month public art exhibition celebrating the International Book Fair in Frankfurt, Germany. Vasquez has lectured on the subject of branding and identity design, and his work has been published in just about every national and international book and periodical on graphic design and advertising.

Robert Matza
Landor Associates,
New York, NY

Eléctrica Bahia, by Oficina de Diseño y Marketing
"Simple, clean, well-balanced positive and negative space, and timeless: all ingredients for a successful mark. The electrical plug is clear and an appropriate message for this company. I was surprised and pleased, at second glance, to discover the hidden letter E. I appreciate the honesty and lack of frivolous decorative noise."

As creative director of Landor Associates New York, Matza brings more than 17 years of experience to his corporate identity clients. In addition to working closely with his design team, Matza collaborates with all other disciplines within the office, including naming, strategy, and new business marketing. Since joining Landor in 1997, he has directed identity programs for Morgan Stanley, GE, PepsiCo, Tenaris, Computer Associates, New York Stock Exchange, Vanguard Group, Lenovo, Cleveland Clinic, Verizon, and Nielsen Media Research. More recently, he built programs for Bristol Meyers Squibb, Citigroup, and IBM. Matza also serves as creative director of Klamath Communications, a specialized group that delivers a full spectrum of integrated communications to select Landor clients.

Prior to joining Landor, Matza spent four years at Chermayeff & Geismar, where he worked with clients such as Sony Entertainment, Telemundo, Mobil Corporation, and Simon & Schuster. He has lived and worked in Madrid, Spain, and through client relationships in South America and Europe he has developed extensive international experience. He holds a BFA in Graphic Design from the Rhode Island School of Design, and volunteers his time and services for many nonprofit organizations.

Kit Paul
Brandient, Bucharest, Romania

Canadian Museum for Human Rights—Winnipeg, for Ralph Appelbaum Associates, by Polemic Design

"This is a piece of work I really admire. The designer achieved a groundbreaking effect by understated, almost humble means, cleverly embedding right into the logo the value this brand stands for: the belief that human rights always come first. Also, I've never seen such a dramatic representation of the truth in Victor Papanek's statement that "design is the conscious effort to impose a meaningful order"—my favorite definition of design seen from quite a literal, unexpected angle."

Cristian "Kit" Paul is a founding partner and creative director of Brandient, the Romanian brand strategy and design consultancy. Before setting up the consultancy with his partners, he cut his teeth on many advertising campaigns and won coveted national and international nominations and prizes while working as an art director and creative director with the advertising agencies Graffiti BBDO, Tempo, and D'Arcy DMB&B in Bucharest. He also worked as a freelance graphic designer in Romania and Singapore. Presently, Paul is deeply rooted in corporate identity while publicly advocating the role of design.

HUMAN RIGHTS CANADIAN MUSEUM FOR

Sharon Werner

Werner Design Werks,
Minneapolis, MN

Mjólka logo, by Ó!
"Smart, simple, memorable, cute. What more could you ask?"

Sharon Werner founded the Minneapolis-based design firm Werner Design Werks, Inc., in 1991. The small studio specializes in combining strong visual language with sound design solutions to create work that affects not only commerce but culture. The office has worked with Target Corporation, Mohawk Paper, Chronicle Books, Mrs. Meyer's Clean Day, Blu Dot Design and Manufacturing, Nick at Nite, VH-1 Networks, Levi's, Minnesota Public Radio, and Moët Hennessey.

Werner's office has garnered national and international awards and honors, and was named the Target Corporation's Vendor of the Year in 2002. WDW's work is included in *100 World's Best Posters* and is part of the permanent collection of the Library of Congress, the Rumpus Room of Ernest and Viola Werner, Musée de la Poste, Victoria and Albert Museum, Musée des Arts Décoratifs, and the Cooper Hewitt Museum.

Initials

D = Design Firm   C = Client

1A D Chimera Design C Victorian Aquatic Industry Council 1B D traci jones design C Creative Alliance
2A D Rule 29 C After 5 2B D Doink, Inc. C Avanti Men's Store
3A D dandy idea C Alexis and Brian Ferguson 3B D Werner Design Werks C Aether for Nike

A B

1

2

3

A B

1

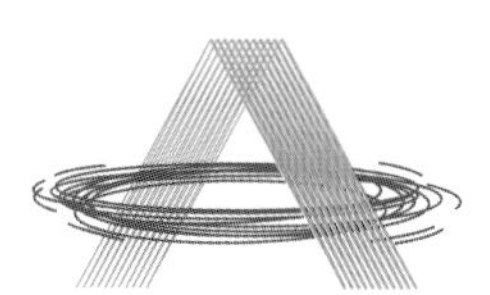

2

3

1A D Strategy Studio C The Armory 1B D Fauxkoi C FauxKoi Design
2A D Roger Christian & Co C Airlume Candles 2B D Steven O'Connor C Allscripts
3A D Lesniewicz Associates C Jamiesons Audio/Video 3B D Pixelube C Artocracy

D = Design Firm C = Client

Initials

Ⓓ = Design Firm Ⓒ = Client

1A Ⓓ The Meyocks Group Ⓒ Agenda One 1B Ⓓ Archrival Ⓒ American Institute of Architecture Students
2A Ⓓ Ikola designs... Ⓒ The Associated Architects 2B Ⓓ Dotzero Design Ⓒ Alternate Universe Events
3A Ⓓ Jason Kirshenblatt Ⓒ A to Z Media 3B Ⓓ Leeann Leftwich Zajas Design Ⓒ The Boston Conservatory

A B

1

AGENDAONE

2

3

A | B

1

2

3

1A Ⓓ Strategy Studio Ⓒ Barton's Chocolates 1B Ⓓ Paul Black Design Ⓒ Burns Service Company
2A Ⓓ Henjum Creative Ⓒ Badger Paper Mills 2B Ⓓ Ikola designs... Ⓒ Brunswick United Methodist Church
3A Ⓓ Landkamer Partners, Inc. Ⓒ Biogenics 3B Ⓓ Steven O'Connor Ⓒ B 10

Ⓓ = Design Firm Ⓒ = Client

A | B

1

2

3

D = Design Firm   C = Client

1A D Ross Hogin Design C Boticelli Pastaworks 1B D Ikola designs... C burningham Weavers

2A D Mindgruve C Blue Motif 2B D Whaley Design, Ltd C Chargo Printing, Inc.

3A D MINE C Blaney Kravitz/Comira 3B D GRAF d'SIGN creative boutique C Cybico

A | B

1

2

3

CAPITALPLAN

1A D Mariqua Design C Clone 1B D AKOFA Creative C Self Promotional
2A D Strategy Studio C Camilli Economics 2B D Werner Design Werks C Chandler Atwood
3A D R&D Thinktank C Capital Plan 3B D Gardner Design C Corry Dance Academy

D = Design Firm C = Client

D = Design Firm C = Client

1A D Jonathan Rice & Company C Champion Energy 1B D angryporcupine*design C Cheryl Dailey
2A D Werner Design Werks C College of Visual Arts 2B D Duffy & Partners C Duffy & Partners
3A D Glitschka Studios C DoodleArchive.com 3B D Pennebaker C Dezyneco

	A	B
1		
2		
3		

A | B

1

2

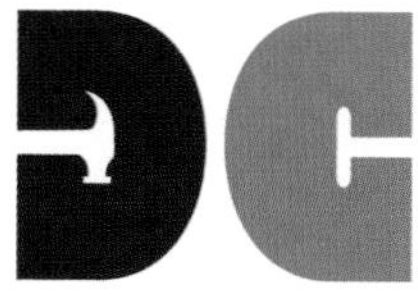

3

1A Ⓓ Lizette Gecel Ⓒ J H I   1B Ⓓ Glitschka Studios Ⓒ DoodleArchive.com
2A Ⓓ Mary Hutchison Design LLC Ⓒ Dow Construction, Inc.   2B Ⓓ GetElevatedDesign.com Ⓒ TheArtFuck.com
3A Ⓓ josh higgins design Ⓒ dk woodcraft   3B Ⓓ concussion, llc Ⓒ Del Lago (Proposed)

Ⓓ = Design Firm   Ⓒ = Client

D = Design Firm   C = Client

1A D Sommese Design C Design Mirage 1B D Exti Dzyn C Print Media & Design, Inc.
2A D joe miller's company C Willow Technology 2B D dmayne design C East Bay Church
3A D Integer Group - Midwest C Ethanol 3B D Morgan/Mohon C Encompass

	A	B
1		
2		
3		

A | B

1

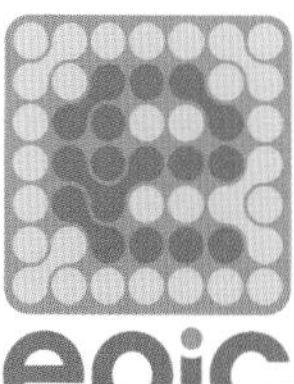

2

3

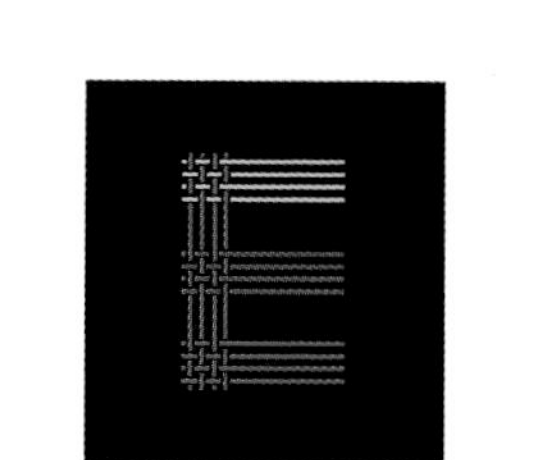

1A Ⓓ Gardner Design Ⓒ EPIC Apparel 1B Ⓓ Ryan Cooper Ⓒ Domenech/etestimonials.com
2A Ⓓ judson design associates Ⓒ Unused 2B Ⓓ Gardner Design Ⓒ EPIC Apparel
3A Ⓓ Paul Black Design Ⓒ Poly Ellerman 3B Ⓓ Zed+Zed+Eye Creative Communications Ⓒ Eric Ebert

Ⓓ = Design Firm Ⓒ = Client

Ⓓ = Design Firm Ⓒ = Client

1A Ⓓ Dotzero Design Ⓒ Ecos 1B Ⓓ Peterson & Company Ⓒ Engenium
2A Ⓓ Brand Bird Ⓒ emerald Graphics 2B Ⓓ FutureBrand Ⓒ Millicom Argentina
3A Ⓓ ODM oficina de diseño y marketing Ⓒ Eléctrica Bahia 3B Ⓓ Diagram Ⓒ E24 Internet Club

	A	B
1	 EFFICIENTPRODUCTS	 ENGENIUM
2	 Emerald **Graphics**	
3		 **E24** INTERNETACTIVE

	A	B
1	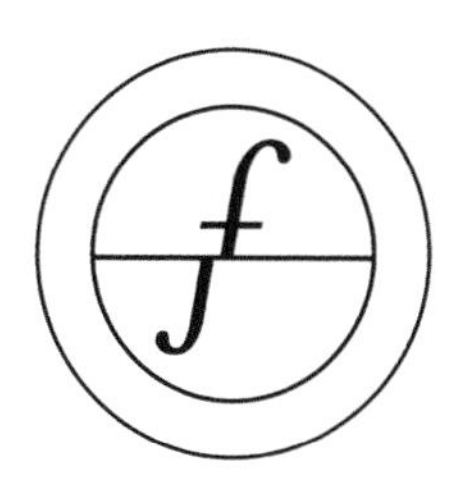	
2		
3	 FascinA	 FAR FETCHED SPIRITS

1A Ⓓ marc usa Ⓒ Fleck Photography 1B Ⓓ Duffy & Partners Ⓒ Thymes
2A Ⓓ McMillian Design Ⓒ Fulton Street BID 2B Ⓓ Mode Design Studio Ⓒ Folinger Mountainwear
3A Ⓓ designlab, inc Ⓒ Weissman's Dance 3B Ⓓ IMAGEHAUS Ⓒ Far Fetched Spirits

Ⓓ = Design Firm Ⓒ = Client

Ⓓ = Design Firm Ⓒ = Client

1A Ⓓ Interrobang Design Collaborative, Inc. Ⓒ FM Group Public Relations 1B Ⓓ Tactical Magic Ⓒ The Eyewear Gallery
2A Ⓓ Allen Creative Ⓒ Grace Fellowship 2B Ⓓ ComGroup Ⓒ ComGroup
3A Ⓓ Diagram Ⓒ Kulczyk Foundation 3B Ⓓ GetElevatedDesign.com Ⓒ Green Lotus Grounds

	A	B
1		
2		
3		

A

B

1

2

3

1A Ⓓ Crackerbox Ⓒ G.W.Engineering 1B Ⓓ Diagram Ⓒ Horyzon Publishing
2A Ⓓ Diagram Ⓒ Horse Publishing 2B Ⓓ Gardner Design Ⓒ Hustler
3A Ⓓ Ross Hogin Design Ⓒ HRCentral 3B Ⓓ Deep Design Ⓒ The Henritze Company, LLC

Ⓓ = Design Firm Ⓒ = Client

D = Design Firm   C = Client

1A D Zed+Zed+Eye Creative Communications C Hilliards Insulation 1B D Dialekt Design C Timex (JDK)
2A D Gardner Design C Hustler 2B D Sibley Peteet C Horizon Printing
3A D Sibley Peteet C Ryan and Dinah Street 3B D Q C Hessen Chemie

	A	B
1		
2		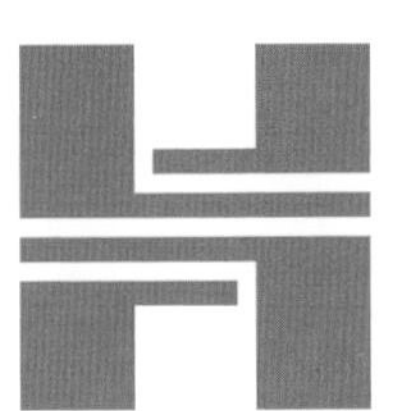
3		HessenChemie

A B

1

2

3

1A Ⓓ Ikola designs... Ⓒ Ikola designs... 1B Ⓓ Ardoise Design Ⓒ Immotik inc.
2A Ⓓ Bryan Cooper Design Ⓒ Impact Productions 2B Ⓓ Sockeye Creative Ⓒ ieLogic
3A Ⓓ Eisenberg And Associates Ⓒ IT Rescue 3B Ⓓ Kendall Creative Shop, Inc. Ⓒ Jarvis Press

Ⓓ = Design Firm Ⓒ = Client

Initials

D = Design Firm   C = Client

1A D Strategy Studio C Jacobs Gardner Office Supply 1B D B.L.A. Design Company C Nathan Good

2A D DDB Dallas C Kemp Academy of Tae Kwon Do and Hapkido 2B D Lesniewicz Associates C Kuhlman Corp.

3A D Funk/Levis & Associates, Inc. C Kelly King & Associates 3B D Diagram C KEA

A

B

1

Jammin' Java Music & Coffee

2

3

Kea Quality Print

A | B

1

2

Landes Investments

3

lenox graphics

1A D www.iseedots.com C Kress Design 1B D Delikatessen C Kontrapunkt
2A D Brandia C Lusomundo 2B D Richards Brock Miller Mitchell & Associates C Landes Investments
3A D Lenox Graphics C Lenox Graphics 3B D Thomas Manss & Company C Metamorphosis

D = Design Firm C = Client

	A	B
1		
2		
3		

D = Design Firm   C = Client

1A D Pixelspace C The Jackson Group   1B D Grapefruit C Mobimax

2A D Idle hands Design C M Digital   2B D FutureBrand C E.Wong-Peru

3A D thomas-vasquez.com C universal music/motown records   3B D Hubbell Design Works C Mavericks Custom Trousers

A B

1

2

3

merchantlogix

1A (D) 68Design (C) Mouton Salon 1B (D) The Meyocks Group (C) Animal Rescue League of Iowa
2A (D) CAPSULE (C) Paladin 2B (D) Misenheimer Creative, Inc/misenheimer.com (C) microinteractive/network 21
3A (D) rajasandhu.com (C) MerchantLogix 3B (D) Simon & Goetz Design (C) Maeser

(D) = Design Firm (C) = Client

A B

1

MetroWest

2

3

Ⓓ = Design Firm Ⓒ = Client

1A Ⓓ judson design associates Ⓒ MetroNational 1B Ⓓ LandDesign Ⓒ Pulte homes, Inc.
2A Ⓓ Gardner Design Ⓒ navential 2B Ⓓ Landkamer Partners, Inc. Ⓒ Nuance Communications
3A Ⓓ Nick Glenn Design Ⓒ Nottingham Demolition 3B Ⓓ designlab, inc Ⓒ cindy Novak

A | B

1

Netscape®

napa valley vintners

2

Notiva

NouvelleVie
Opaque

3

NUANCE AV

orthomol

1A Ⓓ America Online Ⓒ AOL Web Properties 1B Ⓓ Landor Associates Ⓒ napa Valley Vintners
2A Ⓓ Landkamer Partners, Inc. Ⓒ Notiva 2B Ⓓ Dialekt Design Ⓒ Cascades Paper (diesel marketing)
3A Ⓓ Tactical Magic Ⓒ Nuance AV 3B Ⓓ KW43 BRANDDESIGN Ⓒ Orthomol

Ⓓ = Design Firm Ⓒ = Client

	A	B
1		THE OCEAN CLUB
2		
3		

D = Design Firm   C = Client

1A D ODM oficina de diseño y marketing C Oretum 1B D Richards Brock Miller Mitchell & Associates C Presidia Destination Properties

2A D pat sinclair design C HLG 2B D Paul Black Design C Lehndorff Properties

3A D Ammunition C Panchang.com 3B D Robot Agency Studios C Pivot 180 Gear

	A	B
1		
2		
3	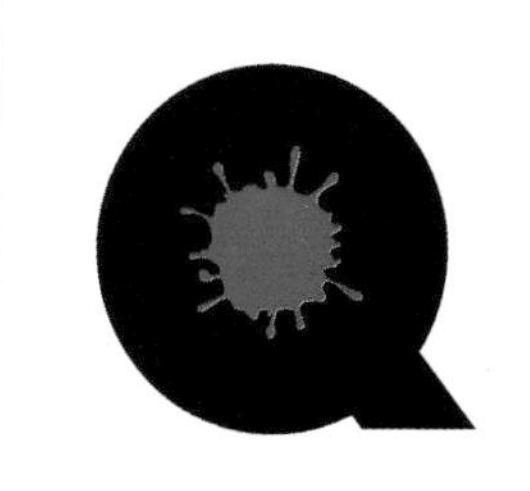	

1A Ⓓ Paul Black Design Ⓒ Pictor 180 Gear 1B Ⓓ Strategy Studio Ⓒ Pace Development Group
2A Ⓓ Steven O'Connor Ⓒ Pascal Hong Interiors 2B Ⓓ R&D Thinktank Ⓒ Quady Painting
3A Ⓓ KOESTER design Ⓒ Q ink 3B Ⓓ ROAD design inc. Ⓒ Pairgain

Ⓓ = Design Firm Ⓒ = Client

Initials

Ⓓ = Design Firm   Ⓒ = Client

1A Ⓓ Fernandez Design Ⓒ TorchQuest   1B Ⓓ Jon Flaming Design Ⓒ Proposed Quark Logo
2A Ⓓ UlrichPinciotti Design Group Ⓒ Quantum Group   2B Ⓓ Wilkinson Media Ⓒ I-Quotient
3A Ⓓ Axiom Design Partners Ⓒ Quality Press   3B Ⓓ Allen Creative Ⓒ River Rehab

A

B

1

2

3

A | B

1

2

3

1A Ⓓ octane inc. Ⓒ Rustad Marketing 1B Ⓓ Edward Allen Ⓒ Revolve Motion
2A Ⓓ Gardner Design Ⓒ Relianz Bank 2B Ⓓ The Meyocks Group Ⓒ rubberdisc.com
3A Ⓓ rajasandhu.com Ⓒ First Rate 3B Ⓓ Rick Johnson & Company Ⓒ Rick Johnson & Company

Ⓓ = Design Firm Ⓒ = Client

Initials

	A	B
1		
2		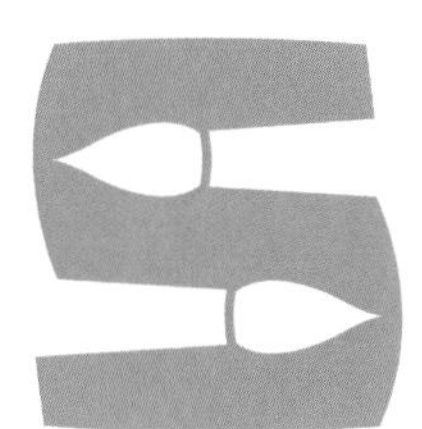
3		

D = Design Firm   C = Client

1A D Gardner Design C Russell Public Relations 1B D Gardner Design C Relianz Bank
2A D Henjum Creative C Oshkosh Symphony Orchestra 2B D Moscato Design C Simpson's
3A D Strategy Studio C Strategy Studio 3B D Gardner Design C Signature Bank 3

A B

1

2

3

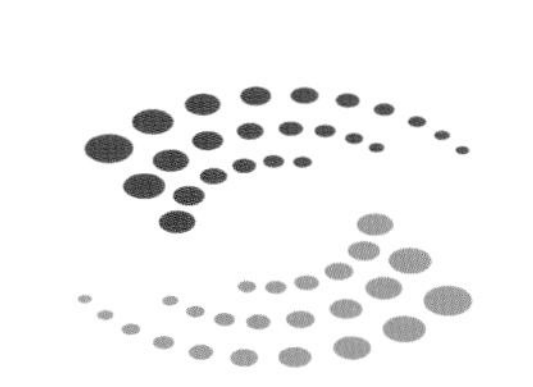

1A Ⓓ Whaley Design, Ltd Ⓒ Sequel Technologies, Inc. 1B Ⓓ Doug Beatty Ⓒ A&P (unused)
2A Ⓓ Pixelube Ⓒ Sara Sutherland 2B Ⓓ Bright Strategic Design Ⓒ Safeway
3A Ⓓ Gardner Design Ⓒ Spectrum 3B Ⓓ Ikola designs... Ⓒ United Methodist Stewardship Program

Ⓓ = Design Firm Ⓒ = Client

Ⓓ = Design Firm   Ⓒ = Client

1A Ⓓ Mires Ⓒ Steve Woods Printing Co. 1B Ⓓ Duffy & Partners Ⓒ Thymes
2A Ⓓ Duffy & Partners Ⓒ Toyota 2B Ⓓ Tchopshop Media Ⓒ Tenon Construction Management
3A Ⓓ Cato Purnell Partners Ⓒ Toll Transitions 3B Ⓓ rehab® communication graphics Ⓒ Unionbay Sportswear

	A	B
1		THYMES
2		
3		

A B

1

2

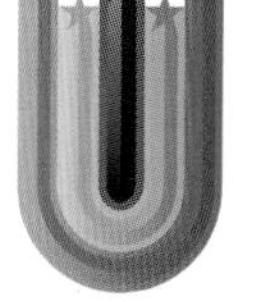

POZNAŃ 2007
UNIVERSIADE

Villa Schneider
turismo, giovani e cultura

3

1A Ⓓ jsDesignCo. Ⓒ United Paint 1B Ⓓ Stand Advertising Ⓒ University Sports Medicine—State University of New York
2A Ⓓ Diagram Ⓒ Universiade Poznán 2007 2B Ⓓ Gabi Toth Ⓒ Villa Schneider
3A Ⓓ Imaginaria Ⓒ Valcasa Properties 3B Ⓓ Sockeye Creative Ⓒ Vero

Ⓓ = Design Firm Ⓒ = Client

D = Design Firm C = Client

1A D Paul Black Design C Voltz Energy 1B D M3 Advertising Design C Ventura Marble

2A D Launchpad Creative C Launchpad Creative 2B D Kendall Creative Shop, Inc. C WestFork Pipeline

3A D Gabriel Kalach*VISUAL communication C W2 Media 3B D Bryan Cooper Design C Wood Window Store

	A	B
1	 VOLTZ ENERGY REGIONAL OIL & GAS	
2		
3		

A | B

1

2

3

1A Ⓓ Jon Flaming Design Ⓒ Watermark Community Church 1B Ⓓ joe miller's company Ⓒ Willow Technology
2A Ⓓ proteus Ⓒ Wellington 2B Ⓓ fallindesign studio Ⓒ Wood Stock Exchange
3A Ⓓ Exti Dzyn Ⓒ Wolfgang Puck 3B Ⓓ maximo, inc. Ⓒ Brooktree Corporation

Ⓓ = Design Firm Ⓒ = Client

Initials

	A	B
1		
2		
3		

D = Design Firm   C = Client

1A D The Joe Bosack Graphic Design Co. C AND 1   1B D Brandia C Audaxys
2A D Brandia C Yorn   2B D Zapata Design C Zapata Design
3A D The Meyocks Group C i wireless   3B D Werner Design Werks C VH1 Network

A

B

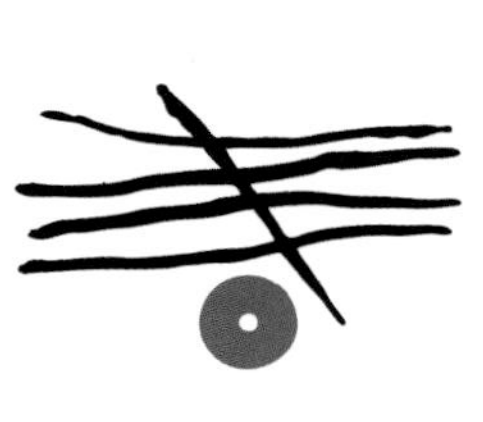

1

2

3

1A Ⓓ ArtGraphics, ru Ⓒ 1 September Publishing House 1B Ⓓ Strategy Studio Ⓒ First Timers
2A Ⓓ 2cdesign Ⓒ Two by Two for Aids and Art 2B Ⓓ Hubbell Design Works Ⓒ Centex Homes
3A Ⓓ Deep Design Ⓒ i3Media 3B Ⓓ Owen Design Ⓒ DSM Art Center

Ⓓ = Design Firm Ⓒ = Client

Ⓓ = Design Firm Ⓒ = Client

1A Ⓓ UNO Ⓒ Minneapolis 1B Ⓓ Direct Design Visual Branding Ⓒ fifth avenue
2A Ⓓ mattisimo Ⓒ Six Stich 2B Ⓓ Chimera Design Ⓒ Tabcorp
3A Ⓓ Day Six Creative Ⓒ Day Six Creative 3B Ⓓ oakley design studios Ⓒ Kink fm 102

	A	B
1		
2	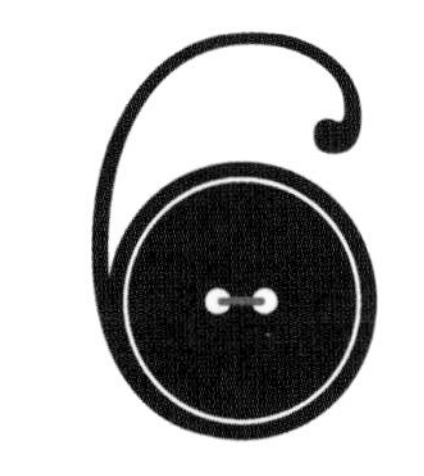	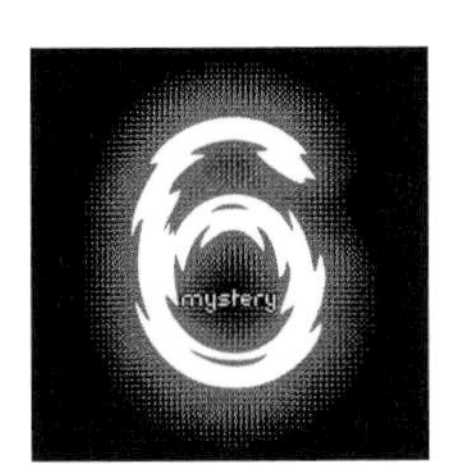
3		

	A	B
1		
2		 elevenfeetmedia
3		

1A Ⓓ Methodologie Ⓒ RC Hedreen 1B Ⓓ GSD&M Ⓒ GSD&M
2A Ⓓ Mindspike Design, LLC Ⓒ Eighth Floor Recording 2B Ⓓ Eleven Feet Media Ⓒ Eleven Feet Media
3A Ⓓ Miles Design Ⓒ Urban Forward 3B Ⓓ judson design associates Ⓒ Unused

Ⓓ = Design Firm Ⓒ = Client

A B

1

41Seventy STUDIO

75 anos BP PORTUGAL

2

3

ReUnion 2001

D = Design Firm C = Client

1A D Shawn Hazen Graphic Design C 41Seventy Studio 1B D Shift design C BP
2A D Edward Allen C 665 Almost Evil 2B D Turney Creative C Momentum Ministries
3A D DDB C 1508 inc. 3B D Aurora Design C Union College Magazine

A | B

1

(poetry center san josé)

2

script:

ink

3

edge

Third point

1A Ⓓ Flaxenfield, Inc. Ⓒ Blo, Inc. 1B Ⓓ joe miller's company Ⓒ Poetry Center San José
2A Ⓓ McGuire Design Ⓒ Script Magazine 2B Ⓓ Kym Abrams Design Ⓒ Ink, inc.
3A Ⓓ MEME ENGINE Ⓒ OMD 3B Ⓓ IMA Design, Corp. Ⓒ Direct Mail Agency Third Point

Ⓓ = Design Firm Ⓒ = Client

	A	B
1	w!se working in support of education	karen hill scott
2	entertrainingEtc educational technologies and consulting	.planum:
3	oyuna	Explore

D = Design Firm   C = Client

1A D Iperdesign, Inc. C Wise 1B D Special Modern Design C dr.karen hill scott co

2A D ODM oficina de diseño y marketing C Entertraining 2B D GRAF d'Sign creative boutique C Planum

3A D Thomas Manss & Company C Oyuna Cashmere 3B D Dotfive C The Luce Foundation—Smithsonian Institute

A | B

1

Velotools

2

seas

3

OBSERVA

1A Ⓓ The Clockwork Group Ⓒ Velotools 1B Ⓓ Ó! Ⓒ FÍT, Association of Icelandic Graphic Designers
2A Ⓓ Kineto Ⓒ Hilton Cebu Phillipines 2B Ⓓ www.iseedots.com Ⓒ Tungsten Design
3A Ⓓ ODM oficina de diseño y marketing Ⓒ Observa 3B Ⓓ thielen Designs Ⓒ Jason Daniello

Ⓓ = Design Firm Ⓒ = Client

Typography

	A	B
1	ZONE	ROTOR
2	40RTY	WINES OF CHILE
3		

D = Design Firm   C = Client

1A D Jejak, rumah iklan dan disain C Zone 1B D Rotor Design C Rotor Design
2A D dandy idea C Texas Commission on the Arts 2B D Future Brand C Wines of Chile
3A D Bakken Creative Co. C Frascati Restaurant 3B D GSCS C Bridge Business partners

	A	B
1	MORGAN HAIR AND SUNLESS TANNING	INDOCHINE
2	WILDFLOWER LINEN	HOME & HABITAT Unique Houston-Hardy Landscapes
3	LUMINA	TRUE STORY

1A Ⓓ Orange Creative Ⓒ Morgan Hair 1B Ⓓ Werner Design Werks Ⓒ Indochine
2A Ⓓ dedstudios Ⓒ Wildflower Linen 2B Ⓓ Times Infinity Ⓒ Home & Habitat
3A Ⓓ judson design associates Ⓒ Lumina 3B Ⓓ NeoGine Communication Design Ltd Ⓒ Stephanie Pietkiewicz

Ⓓ = Design Firm Ⓒ = Client

	A	B
1	CLASSICO	THE MILITARY SHOP
2		I ♡ NY
3		capsul™

D = Design Firm   C = Client

1A D Tiffany Design C Classico Wine 1B D The Design Poole C The Military Shop
2A D Brand Navigation C Island Lodge 2B D Felixsockwell.com C nyc2021
3A D Fredrik Lewander C Dobb Production 3B D Dialekt Design C Toboggan Design

A

B

eurobrAnd
office furniture

1

Da:Da:Da.

white coloured by you

2

clearwire

3

1A Ⓓ jsDesignCo. Ⓒ Throttle, LTD. 1B Ⓓ CAPSULE Ⓒ Lumens
2A Ⓓ ZEBRA design branding Ⓒ Da Da Da 2B Ⓓ Brandia Ⓒ White
3A Ⓓ Hornall Anderson Ⓒ Clearwire 3B Ⓓ Hirshorn Zuckerman Design Group Ⓒ Spa Orange

Ⓓ = Design Firm Ⓒ = Client

D = Design Firm   C = Client

1A D UlrichPinciotti Design Group C Great Lakes Center for Autism 1B D Roger Christian & Co C Warm Springs Rehabilitation System
2A D Peters Design C High Five 2B D logobyte C Brilliant Health Corporation
3A D Stand Advertising C Rich Products 3B D A3 Design C Corkscrew Wine Bar

	A	B
1	the great lakes center for autism	Warm Springs REHABILITATION SYSTEM
2	H!gh F!ve	brilliant corporation
3		corkScrew

	A	B
1	9below	mark. garrison
2	cutcost.com	Institute for Emerging Issues
3	twistology	vessel

1A Ⓓ Brainding Ⓒ 9 Below 1B Ⓓ Vigor Graphic Design, LLC. Ⓒ Mark Garrison Salon
2A Ⓓ Thomas Manss & Company Ⓒ Cutcost.com 2B Ⓓ Polemic Design Ⓒ Ralph Appelbaum Associates
3A Ⓓ Lisa Speer Ⓒ Twistology 3B Ⓓ Blue Storm Design Ⓒ Bystorm

Ⓓ = Design Firm Ⓒ = Client

	A	B
1	bepositive	stepxstep
2	micr°pelt	loglogic
3	(>erb)	pharmacoGenomics

Ⓓ = Design Firm Ⓒ = Client

1A Ⓓ Brandia Ⓒ Galp Energia 1B Ⓓ Lesniewicz Associates Ⓒ Step-by-Step
2A Ⓓ Thomas Manss & Company Ⓒ Infineon 2B Ⓓ Stiles+co Ⓒ LogLogic
3A Ⓓ Eric Baker Design Assoc. Inc Ⓒ verb Interactive 3B Ⓓ Bristol-Myers Squibb Ⓒ Bristol-Myers Squibb

	A	B
1		
2	jantzen	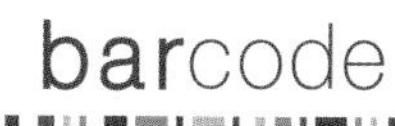
3	mad river post	

1A Ⓓ Chimera Design Ⓒ Astra Lodge 1B Ⓓ Off-Leash Studios Ⓒ Luke O'Malley/Biokorntakt
2A Ⓓ Sandstrom Design Ⓒ Jantzen 2B Ⓓ Bakken Creative Co. Ⓒ Stark Properties
3A Ⓓ sheean design Ⓒ Urban Design 3B Ⓓ label brand Ⓒ Trident Design, LLC.

Ⓓ = Design Firm Ⓒ = Client

Typography

A B

D = Design Firm   C = Client

1A D FutureBrand C Millicom   1B D Liska + Associates Communication Design C Fuse

2A D Corporate Express C Corporate Express   2B D Harwood Kirsten Leigh McCoy C EDS solutions enterprise

3A D Off-Leash Studios C razorfish, inc.   3B D Polemic Design C Michael Reiter

1

fuse

2

n•able

3

HUMAN RIGHTS CANADIAN MUSEUM FOR

	A	B
1	AMNESIA LEST WE FORGET	SHAVED
2	TWIST	CHANGE OF SPACE
3	CREACTIVO	ARSENICO

1A Ⓓ Lars Lawson Ⓒ The Damien Center 1B Ⓓ Polemic Design Ⓒ Shaved
2A Ⓓ mccoycreative Ⓒ Twist Soda 2B Ⓓ Cisneros Design Ⓒ Change of Space
3A Ⓓ brainding Ⓒ Creactivo 3B Ⓓ ODM oficina de diseño y marketing Ⓒ Arsenico

Ⓓ = Design Firm Ⓒ = Client

	A	B
1	NOTORIOUS	PIVOTAL FITNESS
2	EROICA	NEXSYS
3	MUYAKE	SEE-USA

D = Design Firm   C = Client

1A D ZONA Design, Inc C The Biography Channel 1B D greteman group C pivotal fitness
2A D Sharp Communications, Inc. C Eroica Partners LLC 2B D Brand Navigation C Nexsys
3A D Ali Cindoruk C Arredamento Mimarlik 3B D Kym Abrams Design C SEE-USA

	A	B
1		FIVEPOINT
2	LUCINA	
3		

1A Ⓓ Mattson Creative Ⓒ Maroon 5 1B Ⓓ Lisa Starace Ⓒ fivepoint
2A Ⓓ morrow mckenzie design Ⓒ Shauna Mohr 2B Ⓓ Werner Design Werks Ⓒ Skywish for Manhattan Toy Company
3A Ⓓ Miriello Grafico, Inc. Ⓒ Boney's Bayside Market 3B Ⓓ Edward Allen Ⓒ World Uncorked

Ⓓ = Design Firm Ⓒ = Client

	A	B
1	©h®is™as	MARIXA
2	RIVALS	
3	MIKEY	

D = Design Firm   C = Client

1A D Stiles + Co C Christmas 1B D Modern Dog Design Co. C Marixa
2A D Playoff Corporation C Rivals 2B D www.iseedots.com C Hawkins Creative Services
3A D David Kampa C Texas Monthly 3B D batesneimand C Alaska Coalition

	A	B
1	PUSH	BENT
2	SRTECE FTFSU NORTON TFSUF SECRET STUFF™ ERSCET FUFTS TERECS UFTSF	NEW YORK PUBLIC LIBRARY DONNELL BRANCH
3	HŌM	CODY

1A Ⓓ CAPSULE Ⓒ The PUSH Institute 1B Ⓓ Sandstrom Design Ⓒ BENT

2A Ⓓ Gee + Chung Design Ⓒ Symantec Corporation 2B Ⓓ Polemic Design Ⓒ Proposal

3A Ⓓ Interrobang Design Collaborative, Inc. Ⓒ HOM Interior Design 3B Ⓓ Justin Johnson Ⓒ Cody Johnson

Ⓓ = Design Firm Ⓒ = Client

A B

D = Design Firm C = Client

1A D Coleman Creative C Gunn Automotive 1B D Alphabet Arm Design C Kristin Bredimus/Hero Pattern
2A D DDB C Dell 2B D Nita B. Creative C thirst
3A D Kym Abrams Design C North Lawndale Employment Network 3B D Duffy & Partners C Thymes

1

2

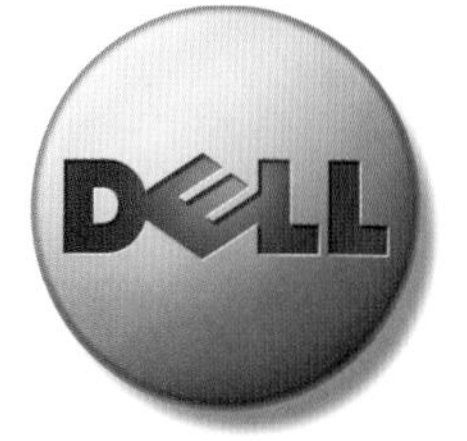

3

	A	B
1		
2		
3		

1A Ⓓ Brand Engine Ⓒ Pixie Maté 1B Ⓓ Campbell Fisher Design Ⓒ Scott Baxter
2A Ⓓ Todd M. LeMieux Design Ⓒ The Bottle Shop 2B Ⓓ Mary Hutchinson Design LLC Ⓒ WOW Baking Company
3A Ⓓ Kaimere Ⓒ Fairmont Hotels 3B Ⓓ KOESTER design Ⓒ Span International

Ⓓ = Design Firm Ⓒ = Client

	A	B
1		
2		
3		

D = Design Firm   C = Client

1A D Design and Image C TalkOn 1B D GSD&M C Chuy's Tex-Mex

2A D Duffy & Partners C Thymes 2B D Alphabet Arm Design C Tim McCoy

3A D sheean design C Cake Productions 3B D David Kampa C Muscletones Sport Wraps

A

B

1

2

3

1A Ⓓ Modern Dog Design Co. Ⓒ Brown Paper Tickets 1B Ⓓ SKOOTA Ⓒ Whiteleaf (proposed)
2A Ⓓ Peterson & Company Ⓒ University of Texas at Dallas School of Management 2B Ⓓ Kern Design Group Ⓒ North Castle Partners
3A Ⓓ NeoGine Communication Design Ltd Ⓒ City Print Communication 3B Ⓓ Parachute Design Ⓒ IVY Hotel + Residence

Ⓓ = Design Firm Ⓒ = Client

Ⓓ = Design Firm Ⓒ = Client

1A Ⓓ GSD&M Ⓒ Austin Museum of Art 1B Ⓓ Landkamer Partners, Inc. Ⓒ Epigram
2A Ⓓ Edward Allen Ⓒ La Zona Rosa 2B Ⓓ www.iseedots.com Ⓒ The Castle Group
3A Ⓓ FutureBrand Ⓒ Avianca Colombia 3B Ⓓ Duffy & Partners Ⓒ Thymes

	A	B
1		iLine
2		
3		

A | B

1

2

3

1A (D) Visual Inventor Ltd. Co. (C) Digimedia 1B (D) Sandstrom Design (C) Fuse
2A (D) Pix Design, Inc. (C) Union Market 2B (D) LogoDesignSource.com (C) INKI
3A (D) judson design associates (C) Story Films 3B (D) Dr. Alderete (C) Spatium magazine

(D) = Design Firm (C) = Client

Enclosures

A B

1

2

3

D = Design Firm C = Client

1A D strategyone C Airgate International 1B D Mirko Ilić Corp C Spread, Inc

2A D Lunar Design C Spider 2B D dale harris C forbean

3A D Sharp Communications, Inc. C Pier Sixty The Lighthouse 3B D NeoGine Communication Design Ltd C Schoc Chocolatier

A

B

1

2

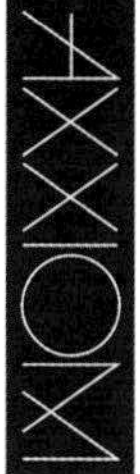

3

1A Ⓓ Tunglid Advertising Agency ehg. Ⓒ KB LÍF 1B Ⓓ Felixsockwell.com Ⓒ felix sockwell
2A Ⓓ SKOOTA Ⓒ Consolidated Shoes 2B Ⓓ Turner Duckworth Ⓒ Refreshment Brands
3A Ⓓ Dotzero Design Ⓒ Portland Metro 3B Ⓓ Church Logo Gallery Ⓒ Church Logo Gallery

Ⓓ = Design Firm Ⓒ = Client

Enclosures

Ⓓ = Design Firm Ⓒ = Client

1A Ⓓ Element Ⓒ element 1B Ⓓ Strategy Studio Ⓒ Bruce Coleman Photo Library

2A Ⓓ Design and Image Ⓒ Joe Hancock 2B Ⓓ Brand Engine Ⓒ inhaus

3A Ⓓ FWIS Ⓒ Readymech 3B Ⓓ Gabriel Kalach *V I S U A L communications Ⓒ Script & Scribble

	A	B
1		
2		
3		

A | B

1

2

3

1A Ⓓ SD Graphic Design Ⓒ Crabtree Lane Studio 1B Ⓓ Bryan Cooper Design Ⓒ Mod Fifties Modern
2A Ⓓ Floor 84 Studio Ⓒ Mr. Kabob 2B Ⓓ morrow mckenzie design Ⓒ New York Tix
3A Ⓓ Living Creative Design Ⓒ WOWOW Entertainments Inc. 3B Ⓓ Ammunition Ⓒ Joe Public Relations Ltd

Ⓓ = Design Firm Ⓒ = Client

Ⓓ = Design Firm Ⓒ = Client

1A Ⓓ The Collaboration Ⓒ The Collaboration 1B Ⓓ Living Creative Design Ⓒ Korea IT Network

2A Ⓓ sheean design Ⓒ Pyramid Creative Studios 2B Ⓓ Alphabet Arm Design Ⓒ Eric Klein

3A Ⓓ Parachute Design Ⓒ RMF Group 3B Ⓓ David Kampa Ⓒ Penny's Pastries

	A	B
1	THECOLLABORATION	
2		
3		

A | B

1

2

3

1A D morrow mckenzie design C Carafe 1B D Fauxkoi C Lily Red
2A D Lars Lawson C The Damien Center 2B D The Flores Shop C Gridlock Paintball Team
3A D Idea Girl Design C Nasty's 3B D R&R Partners C Atomic Testing Museum

D = Design Firm C = Client

	A	B
1		
2		
3		

D = Design Firm   C = Client

1A D greteman group C cosmic cocktails 1B D Werner Design Werks C Style Stretch

2A D Dan Rood Design C John Hutton 2B D Stephan and Herr C Fleer

3A D UNO C Target Stores 3B D Shift design C PTM

A | B

1

2

3

1A Ⓓ S4LE.com Ⓒ Ruby Cruz Ultimate 1B Ⓓ David Kampa Ⓒ Private Clubs Magazine
2A Ⓓ rajasandhu.com Ⓒ Edge Link 2B Ⓓ (twentystar) Ⓒ Oxlo Systems
3A Ⓓ rajasandhu.com Ⓒ rajasandhu.com 3B Ⓓ David Kampa Ⓒ Reebok

Ⓓ = Design Firm Ⓒ = Client

D = Design Firm   C = Client

1A D Iperdesign, Inc. C Nish-Shinjuko, Tokyo 1B D KURT FOR HIRE C Multiverse
2A D GetElevatedDesign.com C People of Diversity 2B D Blue Studios, Inc. C Marvin
3A D Idea Girl Design C Reduce It 3B D judson design associates C k9 Academy

	A	B
1	 flick	post:
2	 pod	marvin
3	 reduce it	ak9demy

A

B

1

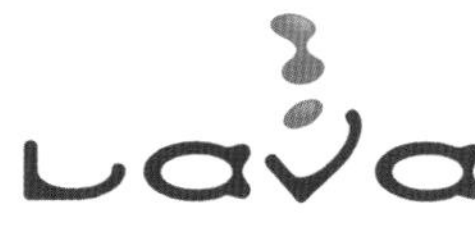

2

3

1A Ⓓ Lance Reed Ⓒ MAF 1B Ⓓ Dialekt Design Ⓒ Toboggan Design
2A Ⓓ Special Modern Design Ⓒ one world 2B Ⓓ Felixsockwell.com Ⓒ Hasbro
3A Ⓓ joe miller's company Ⓒ Businesses United in Investing, Lending, & Development 3B Ⓓ R&R Partners Ⓒ Las Vegas Convention & Visitors Authority

Ⓓ = Design Firm Ⓒ = Client

Ⓓ = Design Firm   Ⓒ = Client

1A Ⓓ Gardner Design Ⓒ Epic   1B Ⓓ Zipper Design Ⓒ Nicola Vruwink

2A Ⓓ dale harris Ⓒ the remedy festival   2B Ⓓ Thielen Designs Ⓒ Hyperactive Music Magazine

3A Ⓓ Studio Stubborn Sideburn Ⓒ Stubborn Sideburn   3B Ⓓ Blacktop Creative Ⓒ Kansas City

	A	B
1		
2		
3		

A

B

1

2

3

1A Ⓓ David Kampa Ⓒ Live Oak Brewing company 1B Ⓓ Delikatessen Ⓒ Stefan Engel Inc.
2A Ⓓ SKOOTA Ⓒ Serious Robots 2B Ⓓ Zona Design, Inc Ⓒ Lenny Kravitz
3A Ⓓ switchfoot creative Ⓒ Fusco Leatherworks 3B Ⓓ element Ⓒ element alternate logo

Ⓓ = Design Firm Ⓒ = Client

Ⓓ = Design Firm Ⓒ = Client

1A Ⓓ Zed+Zed+Eye Creative Communications Ⓒ Rondo's Restaurant 1B Ⓓ M3 Advertising Design Ⓒ navegante group
2A Ⓓ oakley design studios Ⓒ gunther 2B Ⓓ Sam's Garage Ⓒ Sam's Garage
3A Ⓓ M3 Advertising Design Ⓒ Sonny Ahuja 3B Ⓓ Ammunition Ⓒ The Rights Company Ltd

	A	B
1	Rondos	Tolstoys Instruments of Distinction
2	 	
3	 	

A B

1

2

3

1A Ⓓ The Flores Shop Ⓒ Agony Press Publishing 1B Ⓓ nicelogo.com Ⓒ Century City Jazz Festival
2A Ⓓ Steven O'Connor Ⓒ maca 76 2B Ⓓ Chimera Design Ⓒ MOMAC
3A Ⓓ Mirko Ilić Corp Ⓒ darkwood dub 3B Ⓓ Soho Joe Ⓒ KidWise Institute, Inc.

Ⓓ = Design Firm Ⓒ = Client

Ⓓ = Design Firm Ⓒ = Client

1A Ⓓ Strategy Studio Ⓒ Dub Rogers Photography 1B Ⓓ Gridwerk Ⓒ CTN Solutions
2A Ⓓ Garfinkel Design Ⓒ BITS Bunney IT Services 2B Ⓓ Banowetz + Company, Inc. Ⓒ GLAAD
3A Ⓓ Dr. Alderete Ⓒ Gratarola magazine 3B Ⓓ Lisa Starace Ⓒ Chango Macho Hot Sauces

A B

1

2

3

A | B

1

visionworks

2

THE ★★★
NATIONAL
PASTIME

LONG ★ JOHN
SILVER'S

3

CATCH
DESIGN STUDIO

1A Ⓓ Schuster Design Group Ⓒ Visionworks 1B Ⓓ Brandia Ⓒ TAP Portugal
2A Ⓓ Edward Allen Ⓒ The National Pastime 2B Ⓓ Werner Design Werks Ⓒ Long John Silver's
3A Ⓓ Catch Design Studio Ⓒ CATCH 3B Ⓓ pleitezgallo:: design haus Ⓒ La Sierra U. Church

Ⓓ = Design Firm Ⓒ = Client

D = Design Firm   C = Client

1A D Gardner Design C EPIC Apparel 1B D Owen Design C Art 316

2A D JF Studios C 2AM 2B D Stuph Clothing C Toby Mac

3A D Sayles Graphic Design, Inc. C House of Bricks Bar & Grille 3B D Werner Design Werks C VH1 Network

	A	B
1		
2		
3		

A | B

1

2

AP ARTS

3

1A Ⓓ Alphabet Arm Design Ⓒ Or Music 1B Ⓓ Studio Stubborn Sideburn Ⓒ Stubborn Sideburn
2A Ⓓ Edward Allen Ⓒ KAOS—kids are our specialty 2B Ⓓ Banowetz + Company, Inc. Ⓒ Advanced Placement Strategies
3A Ⓓ Hubbell Design Works Ⓒ Ten Restaurant 3B Ⓓ Gabriel Kalach * V I S U A L communications Ⓒ Arrso Restaurants Co.

Ⓓ = Design Firm Ⓒ = Client

A | B

1

2

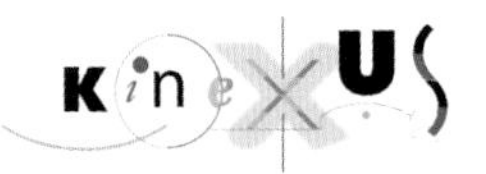

3

D = Design Firm C = Client

1A D Sommese Design C Joe Junk 1B D David Kampa C The Alley Theatre
2A D Peterson & Company C Kinexus Kinetic Museum 2B D Steve's Portfolio C Biblos
3A D rajasandhu.com C Spoiled Rotten Entertainment 3B D Gardner Design C Fringe Salon

A

B

1

2

3

1A Ⓓ soupgraphix Ⓒ Split clothing 1B Ⓓ David Kampa Ⓒ Live Oak Brewing Company
2A Ⓓ David Kampa Ⓒ Loophole Entertainment 2B Ⓓ CONCEPTiCONS Ⓒ Roger Espinoza
3A Ⓓ maximo, inc. Ⓒ Primas de la Viña LLC 3B Ⓓ Whence: the studio Ⓒ Finestra

Ⓓ = Design Firm Ⓒ = Client

D = Design Firm   C = Client

1A D David Kampa C Live Oak Brewing Company 1B D Brian Collins Design C Mimi Dorsey/Fashionrag

2A D David Campa C A Christmas Carol 2B D ROBOT C Botanika

3A D Novasoul C Vaughan 3B D Dotzero Design C Wrapsody Wraps

A

B

1

2

3

A

B

1

2

Lavender

Disfigure

3

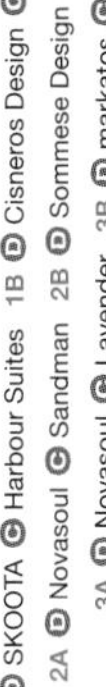

1A Ⓓ SKOOTA Ⓒ Harbour Suites 1B Ⓓ Cisneros Design Ⓒ Anasazi Restaurant
2A Ⓓ Novasoul Ⓒ Sandman 2B Ⓓ Sommese Design Ⓒ Sprouts Inc.
3A Ⓓ Novasoul Ⓒ Lavender 3B Ⓓ markatos Ⓒ Disfigure

Ⓓ = Design Firm Ⓒ = Client

	A	B
1	Lewis and Clark	Spanish Walk
2	Barefoot	Sundance MIND & BODY THERAPY
3	Johnny Reno	Las Vegas

D = Design Firm   C = Client

1A D Rotor Design C Manitou Free Traders 1B D Mattson Creative C Taylor Woodrow

2A D Weylon Smith C Brian and Jannell Barefoot 2B D Octavo Designs C Sundance Mind & Body Therapy

3A D David Kampa C Wildcat Records 3B D David Kampa C Estée Lauder

A B

1

2

3

1A Ⓓ Wray Ward Ⓒ Laseter Seanachai 1B Ⓓ LogoDesignSource.com Ⓒ Fly Label
2A Ⓓ Felixsockwell.com Ⓒ firefly 2B Ⓓ Insight Design Ⓒ Cosmetic Café
3A Ⓓ judson design associates Ⓒ Haute Tuna 3B Ⓓ adbass:designs LLC Ⓒ cobblestoneentertainment grp.

Ⓓ = Design Firm Ⓒ = Client

Ⓓ = Design Firm   Ⓒ = Client

1A Ⓓ Brandesign Ⓒ Sun Tropics 1B Ⓓ Banowetz + Company, Inc. Ⓒ Kent Rathbun/Jasper's Restaurant
2A Ⓓ Abiah Ⓒ Abiah 2B Ⓓ Goldforest Ⓒ QEP Co.
3A Ⓓ Axiom Design Partners Ⓒ Golozi 3B Ⓓ FutureBrand Ⓒ Buenos Aires Provincial Government

	A	B
1	Sun Tropics®	Jasper's
2	abiah DESIGNS	Fresh™ Get Set for Home Décor
3	Golozi GLOBAL CUISINE	PROVINCIA DE Buenos Aires

A | B

1

2

3

1A Ⓓ Lisa Starace Ⓒ ocotillo 1B Ⓓ Dirty Design Ⓒ Noveau Filth

2A Ⓓ NeoGine Communication Design Ltd Ⓒ Schoc Chocolatier 2B Ⓓ Kendall Ross Ⓒ Sukra Yoga

3A Ⓓ Keyword Design Ⓒ Towle Community Theater 3B Ⓓ FUSZION Collaborative Ⓒ United States Conference of Mayors

Ⓓ = Design Firm Ⓒ = Client

Calligraphy

A | B

1

2

3

D = Design Firm   C = Client

1A D CONCEPTiCONS C Zoe-Miniature Schnauzer 1B D Starlight Studio C Miranda Movies
2A D GSCS C UAE royal family 2B D Sakkal Design C M. Al Meer, Dubai
3A D Sakkal Design C Hedgebrook Foundation 3B D Sakkal Design C Tahrir Literary Project

A

B

1

2

3

1A Ⓓ judson design associates Ⓒ Kountry Bakery 1B Ⓓ sheean design Ⓒ Deutsch/LA Advertising
2A Ⓓ Sayles Graphic Design, Inc. Ⓒ Des Moines Jaycees 2B Ⓓ Parachute Design Ⓒ Lusso Exclusive Residence Collection
3A Ⓓ IMAGEHAUS Ⓒ Ron Beining 3B Ⓓ Colle + McVoy Ⓒ CHS

Ⓓ = Design Firm Ⓒ = Client

Crests

Ⓓ = Design Firm   Ⓒ = Client

1A Ⓓ Sockeye Creative Ⓒ adidas 1B Ⓓ Entemotion Design Studio Ⓒ Small Town Treasures

2A Ⓓ Barnstorm Creative Group Inc Ⓒ Mark James Restaurants 2B Ⓓ HMK Archive Ⓒ Mitch Webb & the Swindles

3A Ⓓ Sandstrom Design Ⓒ Full Sail 3B Ⓓ Fauxkoi Ⓒ anodyne bev co.

A

B

1

2

3

A

B

1

2

3

1A Ⓓ Olson + Company Ⓒ Outdoor Corps 1B Ⓓ R&R Partners Ⓒ Ministry of Productivity
2A Ⓓ Gardner Design Ⓒ Fringe Salon 2B Ⓓ Gardner Design Ⓒ Renewed
3A Ⓓ Gardner Design Ⓒ aspen traders 3B Ⓓ dedstudios Ⓒ ecouture

Ⓓ = Design Firm Ⓒ = Client

Ⓓ = Design Firm Ⓒ = Client

1A Ⓓ Sibley Peteet Ⓒ Kenny Wayne Shepherd 1B Ⓓ Gardner Design Ⓒ Renewed
2A Ⓓ Delikatessen Ⓒ Club Nobel 2B Ⓓ Gardner Design Ⓒ Renewed
3A Ⓓ UNO Ⓒ Target Stores 3B Ⓓ eindruck design Ⓒ Ceres Bakery

	A	B
1		Olfactory and Renewed Antique Arts
2		
3		

A | B

1

2

3

1A Ⓓ Design and Image Ⓒ Kamala 1B Ⓓ Dotzero Design Ⓒ Oasis at Bermuda Dunes
2A Ⓓ Wolken communica Ⓒ Avec Amis Event Planning 2B Ⓓ PowerGroove Creative Ⓒ Outwest
3A Ⓓ Ryan Cooper Ⓒ Network Solutions 3B Ⓓ Design and Image Ⓒ Deborah Williams

Ⓓ = Design Firm Ⓒ = Client

A | B

D = Design Firm C = Client

1A D Gardner Design C The Lone Ranger 1B D Garfinkel Design C Bee Natural
2A D Wholesale Distributors C Lucid Inc. 2B Gardner Design C Bradley Paper
3A D Gardner Design C Bradley Paper 3B D judson design associates C Divas

1

est. 1993
BEE NATURAL
ATHENS, GEORGIA

2

3

A	B

1

2

3

1A Ⓓ sheean design Ⓒ Unfiltered Napa 1B Ⓓ Suburban Utopia Ⓒ Downtown Athens Recording Company
2A Ⓓ novle and associates Ⓒ Tyson 2B Ⓓ Barnstorm Creative Group Inc. Ⓒ Central City Brewing Co.
3A Ⓓ Barnstorm Creative Group Inc. Ⓒ Vancouver Police ERT 3B Ⓓ Delikatessen Ⓒ fashion label

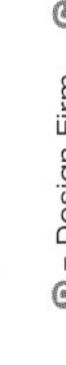

Ⓓ = Design Firm Ⓒ = Client

Crests

	A	B

1

LA COSTA RIDGE

ACHIEVE BALANCE LEAD P SEEK CREATE CHALLENGE INSPIRE ENCOURAGE EXPLORE RESPECT

PEDDIE SCHOOL

2

3

Ⓓ = Design Firm Ⓒ = Client

1A Ⓓ Sabingrafik, Inc. Ⓒ Morrow Development 1B Ⓓ Lippincott Mercer Ⓒ Peddie School
2A Ⓓ Colle + McVoy Ⓒ Greater Minneapolis Crisis Nursery 2B Ⓓ Tactix Creative Ⓒ Pierpont Partners
3A Ⓓ judson design associates Ⓒ Unused 3B Ⓓ Tallgrass Studios Ⓒ Stacey VanHouten

A | B

1

2

3

1A D sheean design C Randall Farm Foods 1B D Tallgrass Studios C Paxico Sausage, Inc.
2A D Steve's Portfolio C SK Designworks 2B D Clark Studios C Travel Channel, USA
3A D fuze C Sierra Tap House 3B D Jonathan Rice & Company C Joshua Experience

D = Design Firm C = Client

A | B

1

2

3

D = Design Firm C = Client

1A D DDB C DDB 1B D SKOOTA C Raleigh Spy Conference

2A D Olson + Company C Bauer Nike Hockey 2B D Gardner Design C Backroads Traveler

3A D Brady Design Ltd C White Castle 3B D Dotzero Design C Lieto

	A	B
1		
2		
3		

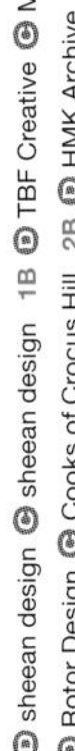

1A D sheean design C sheean design 1B D TBF Creative C Metro Interiors
2A D Rotor Design C Cooks of Crocus Hill 2B D HMK Archive C SharThang
3A D joven orozco design C joven orozco design 3B D RIGGS C Pops

D = Design Firm C = Client

Crests

A B

1

2

3

D = Design Firm C = Client

1A D CDI Studios C Are you Yella? 1B D Gardner Design C The Lone Ranger
2A D Archrival C St. Angelico Gardens 2B D oakley design studios C oakley design studios
3A D CONCEPTiCONS C Bullets and Bracelets 3B D Brand Bird C Tooth & Nail Records

A B

1

2

3

1A D Novasoul C Doc Johnson 1B D Floor 84 Studio C DJ Muggs of Cypress Hill, Soul Assassins for Mash Up Radio
2A D Gardner Design C Material Comforts 2B D Jon Flaming Design C Watermark Community Church ministry program
3A D Richards Brock Miller Mitchell & Associates C Lobo Tortilla Factory 3B D Sayles Graphic Design, Inc. C Carter Printing Company

D = Design Firm C = Client

Sports

D = Design Firm C = Client

1A D The Joe Bosack Graphic Design Co. C NIKE/Arena Football League 1B D The Joe Bosack Graphic Design Co. C Arena Football League
2A D The Clockwork Group C Ozball 2B D Barnstorm Creative Group Inc C Ottawa Renegades CFL
3A D Studio Simon C National Football League 3B D Rickabaugh Graphics C Ohio State University

	A	B
1		
2		
3		

A

B

1

2

3

1A Ⓓ Steve's Portfolio Ⓒ Tierney Communications 1B Ⓓ Glitschka Studios Ⓒ BAM Agency
2A Ⓓ Studio Simon Ⓒ Mudville Nine 2B Ⓓ Studio Simon Ⓒ The Goldklang Group
3A Ⓓ Studio Simon Ⓒ Stockton Ports 3B Ⓓ Studio Simon Ⓒ Minor League Baseball

Ⓓ = Design Firm Ⓒ = Client

D = Design Firm C = Client

1A D Studio Simon C Minor League Baseball 1B D Studio Simon C Modesto A's
2A D Studio Simon C Golden Baseball League 2B D Studio Simon C Long Beach Armada
3A D Studio Simon C Golden Baseball League 3B D Studio Simon C Columbus Catfish

	A	B
1		
2		
3 		

A

B

1

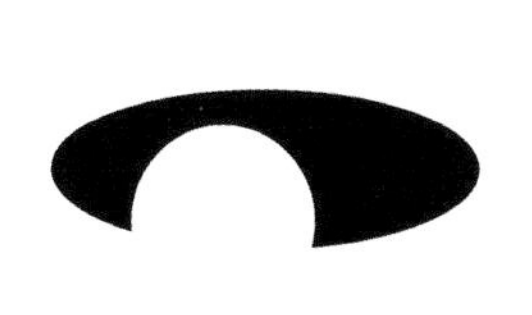

2

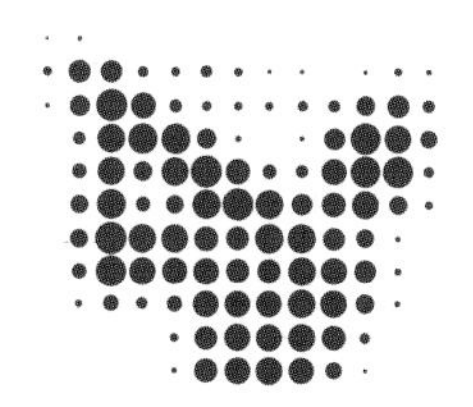

3

1A Ⓓ Studio Simon Ⓒ Yakima Bears   1B Ⓓ Paul Black Design Ⓒ National Hole in One Association
2A Ⓓ The Oesterle Ⓒ the Golf Room   2B Ⓓ b5 Marketing & Kommunikation GmbH Ⓒ GreenSports
3A Ⓓ Jeff Pollard Design Ⓒ Nike   3B Ⓓ Hope Advertising Ⓒ Priddis Greens

Ⓓ = Design Firm   Ⓒ = Client

Sports

A | B

1

2

3

D = Design Firm   C = Client

1A D Edward Allen C Bandon Dunes 1B D Edward Allen C Paloma Loca/Lyon Advertising
2A D Brand Navigation C Puerto Luperon 2B D Mode Design Studio C KT40.com
3A D marc usa C Indpls Sports Corp 3B D Fredrik Lewander C Sprtnik

A

B

1

2

3

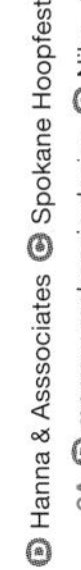

1A Ⓓ Hanna & Asssociates Ⓒ Spokane Hoopfest 1B Ⓓ Sockeye Creative Ⓒ adidas
2A Ⓓ morrow mckenzie design Ⓒ Nike 2B Ⓓ David Kampa Ⓒ Nike
3A Ⓓ David Kampa Ⓒ Nike 3B Ⓓ Rickabaugh Graphics Ⓒ Big East Conference

Ⓓ = Design Firm Ⓒ = Client

Ⓓ = Design Firm Ⓒ = Client

1A Ⓓ Rickabaugh Graphics Ⓒ Ball Hawg 1B Ⓓ Turney Creative Ⓒ Shirts & Skins Basketball
2A Ⓓ Turney Creative Ⓒ Shirts & Skins Basketball 2B Ⓓ Glitschka Studios Ⓒ Kimberly-Clark Worldwide
3A Ⓓ The Joe Bosack Graphic Design Co. Ⓒ Youngstown Steelhounds 3B Ⓓ Barnstorm Creative Group Inc Ⓒ MayDay Marketing

	A	B
1	 	
2		
3		

A B

1

2

3

1A Ⓓ Barnstorm Creative Group Inc Ⓒ Main Events Boxing 1B Ⓓ Diagram Ⓒ Euro 2012
2A Ⓓ greteman group Ⓒ pivotal fitness 2B Ⓓ Synergy Graphix Ⓒ Spring Brothers
3A Ⓓ o2 ideas Ⓒ Vulcan Run 3B Ⓓ The Clockwork Group Ⓒ North Central Rotary Club/San Antonio

Ⓓ = Design Firm Ⓒ = Client

Sports

A | B

1

2

3

D = Design Firm   C = Client

1A D Chimera Design C Tennis Victoria 1B D DDB Dallas C Susan G. Komen Breast Cancer Foundation
2A D humanot C STFC 2B D Eyebeam Creative LLC C America Scores
3A D ComGroup C ADT 3B D Lars Lawson C USA Diving

A

B

1

2

3

1A Ⓓ Lars Lawson Ⓒ USA Diving 1B Ⓓ Braiding Ⓒ Western

2A Ⓓ The Joe Bosack Graphic Design Co. Ⓒ Unused 2B Ⓓ HMK Archive Ⓒ Randall Mays

3A Ⓓ Ross Hogin Design Ⓒ Cutter & Buck 3B Ⓓ Sayles Graphic Design, Inc. Ⓒ American Athletic Incorporated

Ⓓ = Design Firm Ⓒ = Client

Heads

Ⓓ = Design Firm Ⓒ = Client

1A Ⓓ ZEBRA Design Branding Ⓒ Union of Russian Designers 1B Ⓓ ZEBRA Design Branding Ⓒ Rubberman
2A Ⓓ Studio Simon Ⓒ New Hampshire Primaries 2B Ⓓ FUSZION Collaborative Ⓒ Addys
3A Ⓓ Glitschka Studios Ⓒ Work Labs 3B Ⓓ tesser Ⓒ Yum Brands—KFC

	A	B
1		
2		
3		

A | B

1

2

3

1A Ⓓ Steven O'Connor Ⓒ Capleton 1B Ⓓ Sockeye Creative Ⓒ Digital One
2A Ⓓ GRAF d'SIGN creative boutique Ⓒ High Fidelity 2B Ⓓ MEME ENGINE Ⓒ ANYISM
3A Ⓓ Formikula Ⓒ Marc Herold 3B Ⓓ Studio Stubborn Sideburn Ⓒ Stubborn Sideburn

Ⓓ = Design Firm Ⓒ = Client

A B

1

2

3

D = Design Firm   C = Client

1A D KURT FOR HIRE C angry Waiter 4AM 1B D 9fps C 9 Frames Per Second
2A D Kahn Design C Ultimate Rider 2B D Diagram C Von Der Heyden Group
3A D Braindling C Matchstrike 3B D Mattson Creative C Maroon5

A

B

1

2

cameo
Beauty Lounge

3

FACULTY

1A Ⓓ Werner Design Werks Ⓒ Cameo Beauty Lounge 1B Ⓓ GSD&M Ⓒ Gilbert & Sullivan
2A Ⓓ Werner Design Werks Ⓒ Cameo Beauty Lounge 2B Ⓓ Hammerpress Ⓒ the darling room
3A Ⓓ Peterson & Company Ⓒ YMCA Indian Guides 3B Ⓓ Werner Design Werks Ⓒ Textbooks.com

Ⓓ = Design Firm Ⓒ = Client

D = Design Firm C = Client

1A D Dotzero Design C Unicru 1B D FiveStone C Xcentric

2A D Polemic Design C Ryan Rutherford 2B D Straka Dusan C ProSiebenSat.1 Production

3A D Iperdesign, Inc. C PA Virtual Community College 3B D Gee + Chung Design C Give Something Back International Foundation

	A	B
1		
2	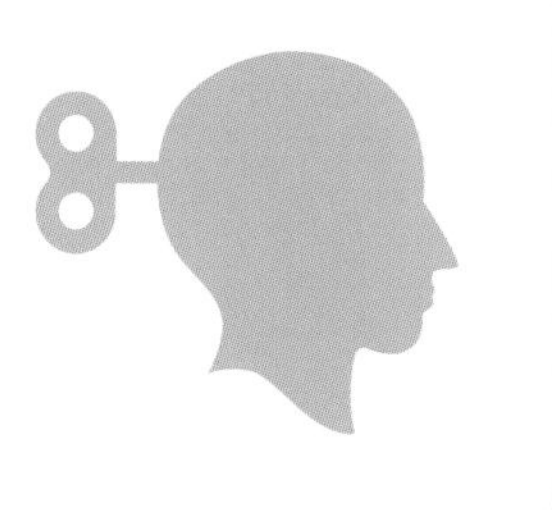	
3		

A

B

1

2

3

1A Ⓓ Felixsockwell.com Ⓒ landor 1B Ⓓ Shelley Design + Marketing Ⓒ W.S. Marketing
2A Ⓓ Gardner Design Ⓒ Chaliss Acquisitions 2B Ⓓ Gardner Design Ⓒ Russell Public Relations
3A Ⓓ CONCEPTICONS Ⓒ Phillip hand 3B Ⓓ Glitschka Studios Ⓒ Glitschka Studios

Ⓓ = Design Firm Ⓒ = Client

Ⓓ = Design Firm Ⓒ = Client

1A Ⓓ Edward Allen Ⓒ Bob Stevens 1B Ⓓ KW43 BRANDDESIGN Ⓒ Dorn im Auge (Charles Greene)
2A Ⓓ Gardner Design Ⓒ The Lone Ranger 2B Ⓓ concussion, llc Ⓒ buckarooart.com
3A Ⓓ Jonathan Rice & Company Ⓒ Pharm To Market 3B Ⓓ Vincent Burkhead Studio Ⓒ the Computer Chef

	A	B
1		
2		
3		

A | B

1

2

3

1A Ⓓ Ross Hogin Design Ⓒ Think 1B Ⓓ UlrichPinciotti Design Group Ⓒ Maumee Valley Habitat for Humanity
2A Ⓓ Glitschka Studios Ⓒ Singapore Design 2B Ⓓ KW43 BRANDDESIGN Ⓒ Ritzenhoff AG
3A Ⓓ Glitschka Studios Ⓒ Studio Presentation 3B Ⓓ Miaso Design Ⓒ Debutante Riot

Ⓓ = Design Firm Ⓒ = Client

Ⓓ = Design Firm Ⓒ = Client

1A Ⓓ Eyebeam Creative LLC Ⓒ The Federal Emergency Management Agency 1B Ⓓ Edward Allen Ⓒ 665 Almost Evil

2A Ⓓ Edward Allen Ⓒ Words & Music 2B Ⓓ Edward Allen Ⓒ 665 Almost Evil

3A Ⓓ CONCEPTiCONS Ⓒ Salvatore 3B Ⓓ rehab® communication graphics Ⓒ rehab® communication graphics

	A	B
1	 	
2		
3		

A | B

1

2

3

1A (D) TBF Creative (C) Valley Forge 1B (D) Werner Design Werks (C) media-MINDS, Inc.
2A (D) UlrichPinciotti Design Group (C) theideakids.com 2B (D) Doink, Inc. (C) The Modern Stage
3A (D) The Oesterle (C) The Oesterle 3B (D) Bryan Cooper Design (C) Bellboy Records

(D) = Design Firm (C) = Client

Heads

	A	B
1	Train Your Brain	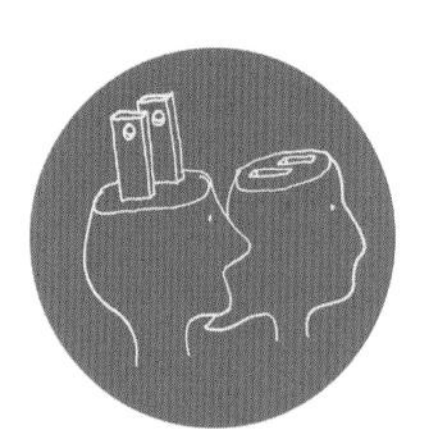
2	 CHILDREN'S THEATRE of CHARLOTTE	
3	 Copasetic Custom Clothing Co.	

D = Design Firm C = Client

1A D MannPower Design C PDI, Inc. 1B D Sommese Design C Sommese Design
2A D Wray Ward Laseter C Children's Theatre of Charlotte 2B D UNO C Vinel Fever
3A D Barnstorm Creative Group Inc. C Copasetic Clothing Co. 3B D Justin Lockwood Design C Avant Garb Clothing

A B

1

2

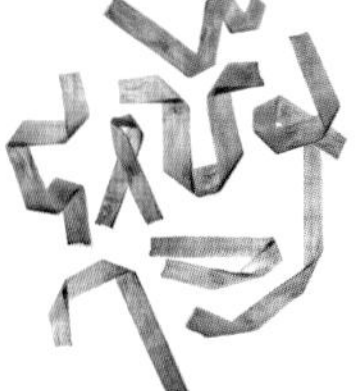

3

1A Ⓓ FUSZION Collaborative Ⓒ Dischord Records 1B Ⓓ Felixsockwell.com Ⓒ AIDS National Quality Center
2A Ⓓ Felixsockwell.com Ⓒ AIDS National Quality Center 2B Ⓓ Glitschka Studios Ⓒ Squiggle-Heads
3A Ⓓ Glitschka Studios Ⓒ Squiggle-Heads 3B Ⓓ Glitschka Studios Ⓒ Colored Man Productions

Ⓓ = Design Firm Ⓒ = Client

A B

D = Design Firm C = Client

1A D Doink, Inc C Caramelo Restaurant 1B D Gee + Chung Design C Virtual Vineyards

2A D Werner Design Werks C Acuity 2B D Glitschka Studios C Persona Global

3A D Jeff Pollard Design C TellThemNow.com 3B D Grapefruit C Rofilco

1

Caramelo
RESTAURANT

Virtual Vineyards

2

3

A | B

1

2

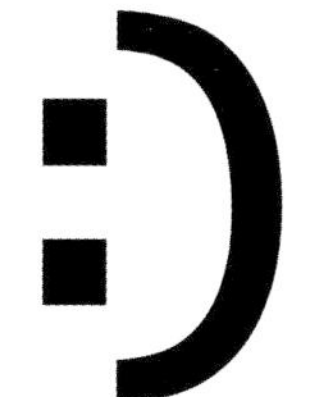

3

1A Ⓓ Werner Design Werks Ⓒ i-Village 1B Ⓓ Turner Duckworth Ⓒ shopping.com
2A Ⓓ thehappycorp global Ⓒ thehappycorp global 2B Ⓓ Les Kerr Creative Ⓒ DynaZeck Technologies
3A Ⓓ Mindspike Design, LLC Ⓒ Dr. James Magestro, Orthodontist 3B Ⓓ David Maloney Ⓒ Brain Magnet

Ⓓ = Design Firm Ⓒ = Client

D = Design Firm   C = Client

1A D Diagram C Ink Design Studio 1B D Braiinding C Papamedia

2A D vincent Burkhead Studio C Collabora Design 2B D Braiinding C Interpretext

3A D J6Studios C Flip Sounds 3B D GSCS C Noshi Noshi

	A	B
1	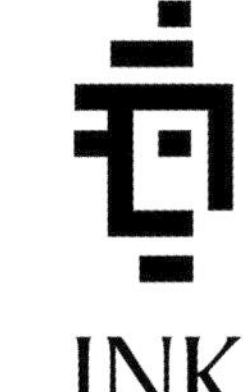	papamedia
2	 Collabora Design	
3		

A

B

1

2

3

1A Ⓓ sharp pixel Ⓒ joe nation 1B Ⓓ V V N Design Ⓒ Brainy Broads
2A Ⓓ Tim Frame Design Ⓒ Tom Maloney 2B Ⓓ Special Modern Design Ⓒ Hype Public Relations
3A Ⓓ Exti Dzyn Ⓒ Egad Dzyn 3B Ⓓ HMK Archive Ⓒ RailYard Productions

Ⓓ = Design Firm Ⓒ = Client

Ⓓ = Design Firm Ⓒ = Client

1A Ⓓ HMK Archive Ⓒ Wild Blue Yonder Entertainment 1B Ⓓ INNFUSION Studios Ⓒ A Maad Tea Party
2A Ⓓ Mariqua Design Ⓒ Lucy Lane 2B Ⓓ Entermotion Design Studio Ⓒ Ad Salon
3A Ⓓ UNO Ⓒ TOO 3B Ⓓ Howling Good Designs Ⓒ Jodi Richards

	A	B
1	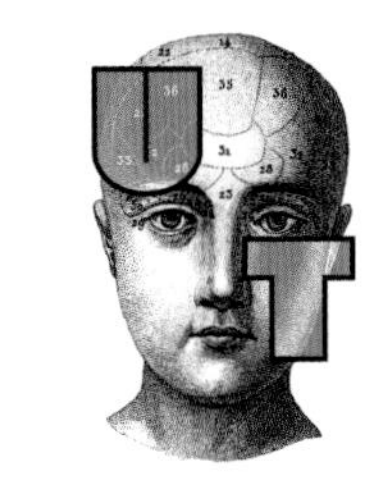	
2	 Lucy Lane	 aD | saLon
3		

A

B

1

2

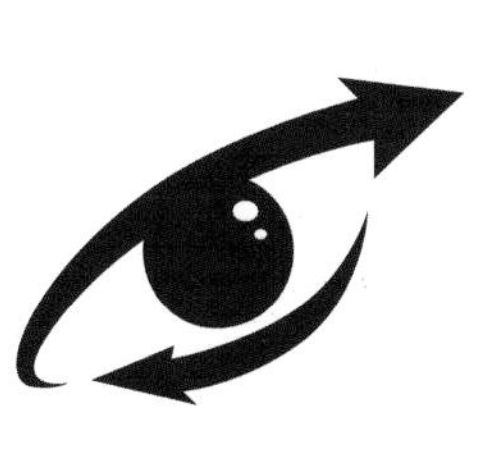

3

1A Ⓓ NeoGine Communication Design Ltd Ⓒ Schoc Chocolatier 1B Ⓓ GingerBee Creative Ⓒ Joy Publications
2A Ⓓ The Clockwork Group Ⓒ Foresight Consulting 2B Ⓓ Ramp Ⓒ Richard Schafer
3A Ⓓ Macnab Design Visual Communication Ⓒ Self/Symbol literacy project 3B Ⓓ Braindng Ⓒ Criterion

Ⓓ = Design Firm Ⓒ = Client

Heads

A | B

Ⓓ = Design Firm Ⓒ = Client

1A Ⓓ i3design Ⓒ Todd Mc Feely 1B Ⓓ Peterson & Company Ⓒ See Pictures
2A Ⓓ Banowetz + Company, Inc. Ⓒ Kim Dawson Talent Agency 2B Ⓓ Chimera Design Ⓒ City of Port Phillip
3A Ⓓ Werner Design Werks Ⓒ Media Minds, Inc. 3B Ⓓ Idle Hands Design Ⓒ Hollyfield

1

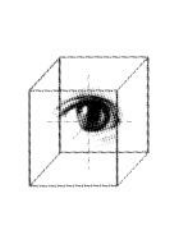

I³DESIGN

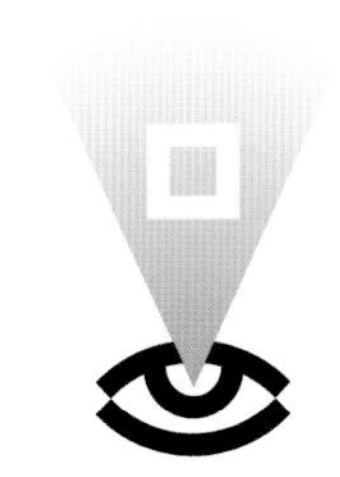

2

3

A

B

1

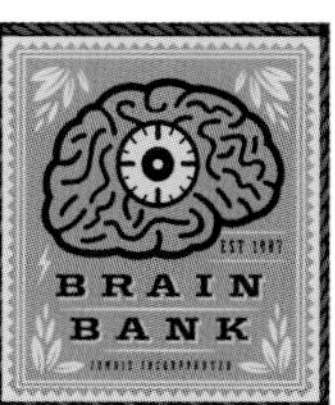

2

3

1A Ⓓ Strange Ideas Ⓒ Brain Bank 1B Ⓓ Turner Duckworth Ⓒ Greenberg Research
2A Ⓓ Special Modern Design Ⓒ Hype 3B Ⓓ Boelts/Stratford Associates Ⓒ Smile Works
3A Ⓓ Brandia Ⓒ Galp Energia 3B Ⓓ GRAF d'SIGN creative boutique Ⓒ MetaCosmetic

Ⓓ = Design Firm Ⓒ = Client

D = Design Firm   C = Client

1A D The Oesterle C Franzz   1B D thomas-vasquez.com C deutsche bank

2A D Matt Everson Design C Ogden Plumbing Co.   2B D Banowetz + Company, Inc. C Total Mail Systems

3A D Miriello Grafico, Inc. C CTB/McGraw-Hill   3B D R&D Thinktank C AGC

	A	B
1		
2		
3	 	

A

B

1

2

3

1A (D) The Oesterle (C) Heidemann 1B (D) The Oesterle (C) Bodymechanics
2A (D) mccoycreative (C) Greener Yard Service LLC 2B (D) The Oesterle (C) Der Ulistrator
3A (D) The Oesterle (C) Eccomonte 3B (D) FUSZION Collaborative (C) September Square Communications

(D) = Design Firm (C) = Client

	A	B
1		
2		
3		

D = Design Firm C = Client

1A D The Oesterle C Eccomonte 1B D R&R Partners C Cowboy Christmas

2A D Banowetz + Company, Inc. C Oz Systems 2B D Element C Columbus School for Girls

3A D nicelogo.com C SICOLAMARTIN 3B D Savage Design Group C Western Lithograph

A B

1

2

3

1A D UNO C Chivas Regal 1B D Hipflix.com C Keystone Auto Shop
2A D 9MYLES, Inc. C RoomKey 2B D Sayles Graphic Design, Inc. C Duane Tinkey
3A D Glitschka Studios C ShipITAPO.com 3B D Peterson & Company C TV Turnoff—Dallas

D = Design Firm C = Client

Ⓓ = Design Firm   Ⓒ = Client

1A Ⓓ Owen Design Ⓒ UA Local 33 1B Ⓓ Macnab Design Visual Communication Ⓒ Long Now Foundation
2A Ⓓ David Kampa Ⓒ Hungry Eye Studios 2B Ⓓ Gardner Design Ⓒ DanseArte
3A Ⓓ Gardner Design Ⓒ Navential 3B Ⓓ Farah Design, Inc. Ⓒ Vzanz Waxing Center

	A	B
1		
2		
3		

A B

1

2

3

1A Ⓓ Chimera Design Ⓒ Hydra 1B Ⓓ FUSZION Collaborative Ⓒ Americans for the Arts
2A Ⓓ Mindspace Ⓒ Chrysalis Shelter 2B Ⓓ GSD&M Ⓒ Our Friends Place
3A Ⓓ greteman group Ⓒ pivotal fitness 3B Ⓓ Kevin France Design, Inc. Ⓒ You're Not Alone

Ⓓ = Design Firm Ⓒ = Client

	A	B
1		
2		
3		

Ⓓ = Design Firm Ⓒ = Client

1A Ⓓ Ross Hogin Design Ⓒ Live Socket 1B Ⓓ Insight Design Ⓒ My Volunteer Center
2A Ⓓ greteman group Ⓒ abode 2B Ⓓ Brandia Ⓒ Multicare
3A Ⓓ Strange Ideas Ⓒ coffee icon 3B Ⓓ Catch Design Studio Ⓒ SunSet Bowling

A | B

1

2

3

1A Ⓓ greteman group Ⓒ connect west 1B Ⓓ motterdesign Ⓒ Viterma
2A Ⓓ SUMO Ⓒ Science City 2B Ⓓ Landor Associates; Ⓒ Lavasa
3A Ⓓ Monster Design Company Ⓒ Now We're Cooking 3B Ⓓ Edward Allen Ⓒ Vespaio Restaurant

Ⓓ = Design Firm Ⓒ = Client

A | B

1

BENNY'S
BAKERY

2

3

D = Design Firm C = Client

1A D HMK Archive C Igloo Group Austin 1B D Stephan and Herr C Benny's Bakery
2A D Banowetz + Company, Inc. C Wall's Catering 2B D Designsensory C Eddies Pizza
3A D Straka Dusan C CoFee (Bar/Restaurant) 3B D NeoGine communication Design Ltd C Van Dyck Fine Foods

	A	B
1		
2		
3		

1A Ⓓ Glitschka Studios Ⓒ Kimberly-Clark Worldwide 1B Ⓓ Felixsockwell.com Ⓒ esquire book club
2A Ⓓ Werner Design Werks Ⓒ H.D.M.G. 2B Ⓓ Idle hands Design Ⓒ Drexel
3A Ⓓ Launchpad Creative Ⓒ Red Handle Pictures 3B Ⓓ Paul Black Design Ⓒ Jensen Magic

Ⓓ = Design Firm Ⓒ = Client

D = Design Firm   C = Client

1A D 343 Creative C Atlas Welding 1B D Diagram C Strongpage

2A D Formikula C Yakuza Attack Dog—Asian MoviesWebsite 2B D Werner Design Werks C Cameo Beauty Lounge

3A D Launchpad Creative C Isabella 3B D Paul Black Design C Brandye James

	A	B
1	atlas WELDING AND BOILER REPAIR	
2		
3	 	

A B

1

2

3

Corporate Challenge

1A Ⓓ Edward Allen Ⓒ Ranger Construction 1B Ⓓ Edward Allen Ⓒ Glazing Saddles LTD
2A Ⓓ Boelts/Stratford Associates Ⓒ Big Rays Restaurant 2B Ⓓ Maremar Graphic Design Ⓒ Bob Leith
3A Ⓓ Harwood Kirsten Leigh McCoy Ⓒ Lemnos Dubai 3B Ⓓ Bryan Cooper Design Ⓒ WorldCom

Ⓓ = Design Firm Ⓒ = Client

People

A B

1

2

3

D = Design Firm C = Client

1A D Jonathan Rice & Company C Grapevine High School 1B D Formikula C Marc Herold
2A D Vincent Burkhead Studio C Primm & Partners 2B D David Kampa C Pamela Hawthorne
3A D Strange Ideas C stop design theft! 3B D Sabingrafik, Inc. C Settlers Ridge

A

B

1

2

3

1A D greteman group C art 101 1B D Straka Dusan C Festundfrei eK
2A D Dotzero Design C Kritis 2B D Dotzero Design C PCM
3A D FUSZION Collaborative C F&W Publications 3B D Insight Design C Single Source

D = Design Firm C = Client

D = Design Firm C = Client

1A D The Gate C HelaCapital 1B D Richards Brock Miller Mitchell & Associates C Champion Contractors
2A D Visual Inventor Ltd. Co. C Tulsa Radiology Associates/Visionmakers 2B D cc design C Narcissus
3A D 9MYLES, Inc. C Alignment in Motion 3B D Bronson Ma Creative C Inner City Relief

	A	B
1	 	
2		
3		

	A	B
1		
2		
3		

1A Ⓓ Strange Ideas Ⓒ secret perfume 1B Ⓓ Dotzero Design Ⓒ Polish Festival
2A Ⓓ Werner Design Werks Ⓒ VH1 Network 2B Ⓓ Diagram Ⓒ Wedliniarnia Meat Delicatessen
3A Ⓓ HMK Archive Ⓒ Sabas Trio International 3B Ⓓ GS&M Ⓒ Joy Moves

Ⓓ = Design Firm Ⓒ = Client

Ⓓ = Design Firm Ⓒ = Client

1A Ⓓ Zwölf Sonnen Ⓒ Einwohner und Integrationsamt Wiesbaden 1B Ⓓ Jon Flaming Design Ⓒ Connecting Point
2A Ⓓ Lance Reed Ⓒ Soho 2B Ⓓ joven orozco design Ⓒ Barcode Guys
3A Ⓓ Campbell Fisher Design Ⓒ Pot Heads 3B Ⓓ humanot Ⓒ Unseen Kings

	A	B
1		
2		
3		

	A	B
1		
2		
3		

1A Ⓓ Wolken communica Ⓒ Just Cauz 1B Ⓓ DDB Dallas Ⓒ Milton Development Company
2A Ⓓ Communique Ⓒ Foster the Future 2B Ⓓ (twentystar) Ⓒ Colorado Ridge Church
3A Ⓓ Zwölf Sonnen Ⓒ Peter Kohl 3B Ⓓ Launchpad Creative Ⓒ Daisy Group

Ⓓ = Design Firm Ⓒ = Client

D = Design Firm   C = Client

1A D Monster Design Company C Milkdrunk Baby   1B D Idle Hands Design C Luna Ladder Art for Productions, LLC

2A D Glitschka Studios C Glitschka Studios   2B D Gabi Toth C Conti Grup Romania

3A D M3 Advertising Design C Chris Hammond   3B D Studio D C Glen Burtnik

	A	B
1	 MILKDRUNK BABY	
2		
3		

A

B

1

2

3

1A Ⓓ Who's the Min / Creative Solutions Ⓒ BandCamp Productions 1B Ⓓ Mattson Creative Ⓒ Vital Dynamics
2A Ⓓ i4 Solutions Ⓒ Ron Williams 2B Ⓓ Farm Design Ⓒ Street Jammy Jam Series
3A Ⓓ J6Studios Ⓒ Houston Area Knife Stickers 3B Ⓓ Element Ⓒ Soul Theater Productions

Ⓓ = Design Firm  Ⓒ = Client

	A	B
1	 	
2		
3		

Ⓓ = Design Firm Ⓒ = Client

1A Ⓓ greteman group Ⓒ BigInk 1B Ⓓ Project center Ⓒ Motorhead Automotive
2A Ⓓ Felixsockwell.com Ⓒ FedEx 2B Ⓓ STUN Design and Advertising Ⓒ Exposure Control
3A Ⓓ Stoltze Design Ⓒ Chelsea Pictures 3B Ⓓ Sabet Branding Ⓒ Agile Health Services

A | B

1

URA

UPSTATE RESTORATION
INCORPORATED

2

3

1A Ⓓ RIGGS Ⓒ Upstate Restoration, Inc. 1B Ⓓ Hubbell Design Works Ⓒ Weiser Films
2A Ⓓ Blue Tricycle, Inc. Ⓒ Big Daddy, Inc. 2B Ⓓ Felixsockwell.com Ⓒ HRC
3A Ⓓ Glitschka Studios Ⓒ Persona Global 3B Ⓓ FUSZION Collaborative Ⓒ Shake Your Booty

Ⓓ = Design Firm Ⓒ = Client

D = Design Firm   C = Client

1A D Shift design C ACP   1B D Sayles Graphic Design, Inc. C Principle Financial Group

2A D Ardoise Design C Centre de répit Philou   2B D Stacy Bormett Design, LLC C Ideation Factory

3A D Jeff Pollard Design C Wanker's Corner   3B D The Oesterle C T-Shock—Die Hemdenlegion

	A	B
1		
2		
3		

A | B

1

2

3

1A D Glitschka Studios C BAM Agency 1B D BCM/D C Scott Mescher
2A D mixdesign C T.J. Maloney's 2B D Dr.Alderete C Plan 9 store
3A D CH&LER Design C By the Cup 3B D Werner Design Werks C Cameo Beauty Lounge

D = Design Firm C = Client

A | B

1

2

3

D = Design Firm   C = Client

1A D Red Circle C Stardome Golf Center 1B D Fresh Oil C Rhode Runner
2A D Straka Dusan C Warner Music/ProSiebenSat.1 Media AG 2B D www.iseedots.com C Badhusid
3A D Werner Design Werks C TvbyGirls 3B D R&D Thinktank C FirstFlight

A

B

1

2

3

1A D Edward Allen C Upstairs 1B D Les Kerr Creative C Visibility, Inc.
2A D Justin Lockwood Design C Artattack Theater 2B D mccoycreative C Marc Vecco Marine Photography
3A D Felixsockwell.com C Coca-Cola 3B D David Kampa C Communities in Schools

D = Design Firm C = Client

A | B

Ⓓ = Design Firm Ⓒ = Client

1A Ⓓ Les Kerr Creative Ⓒ People Results 1B Ⓓ Ammunition Ⓒ Weber-Shandwick Worldwide
2A Ⓓ 02 ideas Ⓒ 94.5 2B Ⓓ Howerton+White Interactive Ⓒ Maternal Fetal Associates of Kansas
3A Ⓓ Strange Ideas Ⓒ connect mate 3B Ⓓ elf design Ⓒ Weddings

1

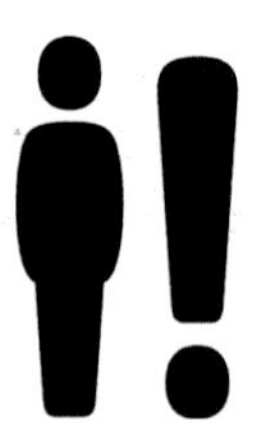

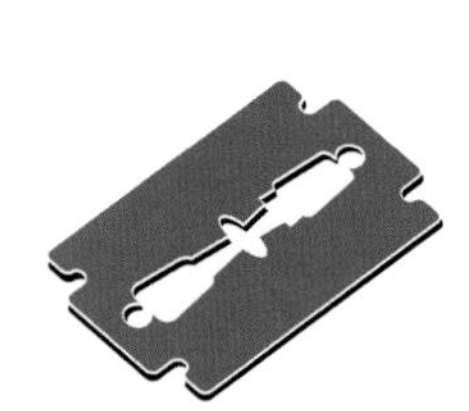

2

3

A | B

1

2

DOUBLE ANGEL FOUNDATION

3

1A Ⓓ Felixsockwell.com Ⓒ AIDS National Quality Center 1B Ⓓ Straka Dusan Ⓒ residential home for the elderly
2A Ⓓ Straka Dusan Ⓒ FirstFootStep 2B Ⓓ BrandSavvy, Inc. Ⓒ Double Angel Foundation
3A Ⓓ FUSZION Collaborative Ⓒ abyan.com 3B Ⓓ Shelley Design + Marketing Ⓒ Parents Anonymous

Ⓓ = Design Firm Ⓒ = Client

D = Design Firm   C = Client

1A D UNO C Kimberly Clark 1B D traci jones design C Hearts for Forgotten Angels
2A D Sommese Design C Children's Playschool 2B D monster design C Microsoft Alumni Association
3A D Macnab Design Visual Communication C Insight Out 3B D Kevin France Design, Inc. C You're Not Alone

	A	B
1		
2		msa MICROSOFT®ALUMNI NETWORK
3		

A

B

1

2

3

1A Ⓓ o2 ideas Ⓒ Quorum 1B Ⓓ Special Modern Design Ⓒ Flewelling & Moody Architects
2A Ⓓ McAndrew Kaps Ⓒ Associated Pension Service 2B Ⓓ Peterson & Company Ⓒ ERF (Employees' Retirement Fund of the City of Dallas)
3A Ⓓ Lesniewicz Associates Ⓒ Marrow Donor 3B Ⓓ Howerton + White Interactive Ⓒ hart

Ⓓ = Design Firm Ⓒ = Client

A | B

1

2

3

D = Design Firm   C = Client

1A D Stiles + co C Adventure Music/KLIU radio 1B D Felixsockwell.com C ncayv
2A D Gardner Design C Russell Public Relations 2B D Shift design C BP
3A D Oxide Design Co. C Nebraska AIDS Project 3B D zengigi design C Ogilvy PR

A

B

1A D Edward Allen C Force of Nature Organization 1B D GRAF d'SIGN creative boutique C Polittech
2A D Grapefruit C Velfina 2B D Perfect Circle Media Group C Red cross International
3A D o2 ideas C Hand in Paw Animal Therapy 3B D Werner Design Werks C Textbooks.com

D = Design Firm C = Client

	A	B
1	 	
2		
3		

Ⓓ = Design Firm Ⓒ = Client

1A Ⓓ Polemic Design Ⓒ Expert Construction, LLC 1B Ⓓ Gabriel Kalach * V I S U A L communications Ⓒ Media Targets
2A Ⓓ thomas-vasquez.com Ⓒ Viacom/Rock the Vote 2B Ⓓ Werner Design Werks Ⓒ Media Minds, Inc.
3A Ⓓ nicelogo.com Ⓒ University of Texas 3B Ⓓ Design and Image Ⓒ LifeSpark

	A	B
1		
2		
3		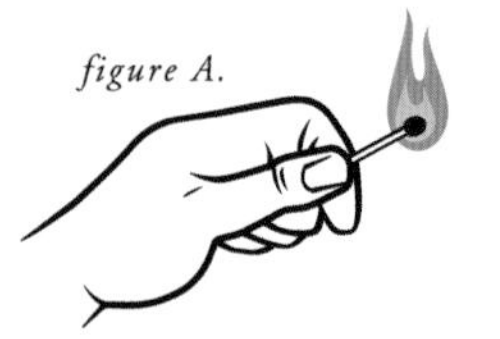

1A Ⓓ designlab, inc Ⓒ Spa of Eden 1B Ⓓ Werner Design Werks Ⓒ Acuity
2A Ⓓ Fauxkoi Ⓒ CatLick Records 2B Ⓓ Peterson & Company Ⓒ Simply Placed
3A Ⓓ Doug Beatty Ⓒ A&P (unused) 3B Ⓓ Ross Hogin Design Ⓒ Strikeplate

Ⓓ = Design Firm Ⓒ = Client

D = Design Firm C = Client

1A D Insomniac Creative Studio C Invercity/Ben Bisbee 1B D Edward Allen C Code Warrior

2A D MEME ENGINE C YCLUSA 2B D Element C Intervarsity, Vineyard Church

3A D Visual Inventor Ltd. Co. C Addington Baptist Church 3B D Bronson Ma Creative C Reverse Mortgage Texas

	A	B
1		
2		
3		

	A	B
1		
2	NORDSEE PFLEGE MIT HERZ & HAND	
3		

1A Ⓓ Gabi Toth Ⓒ Hotel Unirea 1B Ⓓ Carol Gravelle Graphic Design Ⓒ CaraMina Inc. 2A Ⓓ Braue; Branding & Corporate Design Ⓒ NordseePflege
2B Ⓓ Banowetz + Company, Inc. Ⓒ Love Chiropractic 3A Ⓓ Macnab Design Visual Communication Ⓒ Southwest Cardiology Associates
3B Ⓓ Yellow Pencil Brand Sharpening Ⓒ Canterbury West Coast Air Rescue Trust

Ⓓ = Design Firm Ⓒ = Client

People

	A	B
1		
2		
3		

D = Design Firm C = Client

1A D Polemic Design C Pax Christi Metro New York 1B D Sire Advertising C Sozo Healing Arts
2A D stressdesign C Clayscapes Pottery, LLC 2B D Univisual C VistaSi
3A D Macnab Design Visual Communication C Body Wisdom Day Spa 3B D mccoycreative C HandsOn Salon

A B

1

2

3

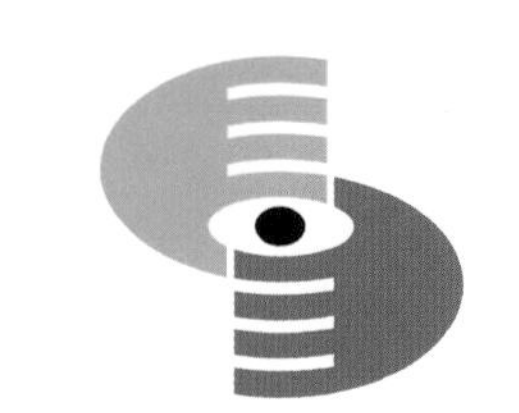

1A Ⓓ FigDesign Ⓒ Webb Chiropractic 1B Ⓓ Think Tank Creative Ⓒ Acadiana Open Channel
2A Ⓓ Jenny Kolcun Freelance Designer Ⓒ Ojo Photography 2B Ⓓ Peterson & Company Ⓒ Women's National Book Association
3A Ⓓ Jeff Pollard Design Ⓒ Digitech Solutions 3B Ⓓ Garfinkel Design Ⓒ International Service Public Outreach

Ⓓ = Design Firm Ⓒ = Client

Ⓓ = Design Firm Ⓒ = Client

1A Ⓓ Fuego3 Ⓒ Dove Counseling Services 1B Ⓓ Harkey Design Ⓒ Harkey Design
2A Ⓓ FUSZION Collaborative Ⓒ CADCA 2B Ⓓ Glitschka Studios Ⓒ Glitschka Studios
3A Ⓓ Atha Design Ⓒ Oskaloosa Elementary PTO 3B Ⓓ Gabriela Gasparini Design Ⓒ Colby & Partners

	A	B
1		
2		
3		

	A	B
1		
2		
3		

1A Ⓓ Glitschka Studios Ⓒ GloveMobile.com 1B Ⓓ Kahn Design Ⓒ Kathy Taylor/Acupuncture & Chinese Herbalist
2A Ⓓ Felixsockwell.com Ⓒ Cigna 2B Ⓓ IMA Design, Corp. Ⓒ Club Portfelio
3A Ⓓ Felixsockwell.com Ⓒ Cigna 3B Ⓓ Idea Girl Design Ⓒ Special Olympics

Ⓓ = Design Firm Ⓒ = Client

	A	B
1		
2		
3		

D = Design Firm C = Client

1A D Iperdesign, Inc. C De Carolis Jewelry 1B D Farah Design, Inc. C Farah Design
2A D V V N Design C Influence 2B D Sommese Design C Penn State Jazz Club
3A D KW43 BRANDDESIGN C Ritzenhoff AG 3B D Sabingrafik, Inc. C Hot Rod Hell

A B

1

2

3

1A Ⓓ Scott Oeschger Design Ⓒ Scott Oeschger 1B Ⓓ Tactix Creative Ⓒ Work Labs
2A Ⓓ GSD&M Ⓒ Tabacco Beast 2B Ⓓ Werner Design Werks Ⓒ i-Village
3A Ⓓ Tactix Creative Ⓒ www.BadDesignKills.com 3B Ⓓ Glitschka Studios Ⓒ BadDesignKills.com

Ⓓ = Design Firm Ⓒ = Client

A B

1

2

3

D = Design Firm   C = Client

1A D Edward Allen C Hellbillies 1B D Zed+Zed+Eye Creative Communications C Matt Villella
2A D Glitschka Studios C Haro Bikes 2B D sheean design C Triathlete Zombies
3A D Novasoul C Legion 3B D Dotzero Design C FrightTown

A | B

1

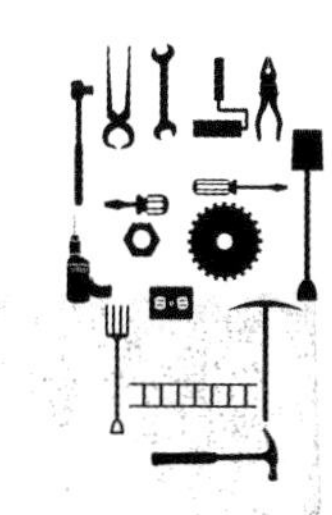

2

3

1A Ⓓ DDB Ⓒ The Home Depot 1B Ⓓ The Oesterle Ⓒ Spika In Snüzz
2A Ⓓ R&D thinktank Ⓒ Public Executions 2B Ⓓ Rome & Gold Creative Ⓒ Gold Medal Swim Camp
3A Ⓓ Monster Design Company Ⓒ Monster Design Company 3B Ⓓ Ross Hogin Design Ⓒ Storm Hockey Camps

Ⓓ = Design Firm Ⓒ = Client

A

B

1

2

3

D = Design Firm   C = Client

1A D Dotzero Design C FrightTown 1B D FWIS C Squarewolf
2A D Ammunition C Lovechild 2B D o2 ideas C Vagos Restaurant
3A D markatos C Disfigure 3B D Special Modern Design C Jennifer Diamond Foundation

A	B	
		1
	 TWO SAINTS estate winery	2
		3

1A Ⓓ Olson + Company Ⓒ The Basilica of St. Mary 1B Ⓓ concussion, llc Ⓒ Recommended Foods, Inc.
2A Ⓓ Lisa Starace Ⓒ all my sons 2B Ⓓ The Meyocks Group Ⓒ Two Saints
3A Ⓓ Pixel Basement Ⓒ Tav Shande 3B Ⓓ R&D Thinktank Ⓒ Delta Medics

Ⓓ = Design Firm Ⓒ = Client

A B

1

2

3

Ⓓ = Design Firm Ⓒ = Client

1A Ⓓ Gardner Design Ⓒ ESSFA 1B Ⓓ Macnab Design Visual Communication Ⓒ Angela Buono

2A Ⓓ CAPSULE Ⓒ Myth Nightclub 2B Ⓓ McAndrew Kaps Ⓒ Wavecode

3A Ⓓ Gardner Design Ⓒ Spirit Aerosystems 3B Ⓓ Tactical Magic Ⓒ Fulmer Helmets

A | B

1

Shibboleth

2

THE GRIFFIN.COMPANY

3

PEGASUS

1A Ⓓ Hinge Ⓒ Internet2 1B Ⓓ ivan2design Ⓒ Kharakat
2A Ⓓ Harkey Design Ⓒ Griffin Company 2B Ⓓ David Kampa Ⓒ Horsefeathers Trading Company
3A Ⓓ Quest Fore Ⓒ GlaxoSmithKline 3B Ⓓ Element Ⓒ Columbus School for Girls

Ⓓ = Design Firm Ⓒ = Client

A | B

1

horn

złote tarasy

2

3

D = Design Firm   C = Client

1A D Diagram C ING Real Estate Development 1B D Sergio Bianco C Incisori Fiorentini

2A D Idle Hands Design C Ouroboros Ink 2B D Turner Duckworth C S.A. Brain & Co. Ltd

3A D Glitschka Studios C Body Glove—Asia 3B D Studio Simon C Golden Baseball League

A | B

1

2

3

1A Ⓓ the atmosfear Ⓒ MGM MIRAGE 1B Ⓓ www.iseedots.com Ⓒ Novastor
2A Ⓓ sheean design Ⓒ Maddocks & Co. 2B Ⓓ Sommese Design Ⓒ Penn State Jazz Club
3A Ⓓ Ramp Ⓒ Kelston International 3B Ⓓ Diagram Ⓒ ING Real Estate Development

Ⓓ = Design Firm Ⓒ = Client

A | B

1

MERCUITY

2

3

D = Design Firm   C = Client

1A D Tim Frame Design C Crashshop 1B D ASGARD C Shell Company 78
2A D Rotor Design C Ames Children's Theater 2B D Fuze C akaKeen
3A D Werner Design Werks C Aether for Nike 3B D Tactix Creative C Boat Locker

A | B

1

2

3

1A Ⓓ Glitschka Studios Ⓒ Rearden Studio 1B Ⓓ Glitschka Studios Ⓒ Publisher
2A Ⓓ Glitschka Studios Ⓒ Publisher 2B Ⓓ Glitschka Studios Ⓒ Publisher
3A Ⓓ Dr. Alderete Ⓒ Heineken Mexico 3B Ⓓ Fuego3 Ⓒ Fuego3

Ⓓ = Design Firm Ⓒ = Client

D = Design Firm   C = Client

1A D Tactix Creative C Moki's 1B D Fifth Letter C Ooga Booga!, Inc.
2A D Glitschka Studios C Upper Deck Company 2B D Chad Carr Design C Space Cat
3A D CONCEPTiCONS C Migdia Chinea 3B D Strange Ideas C pop robot icon

	A	B
1	Moki's SURF SHACK	
2		
3		

A | B

1

2

3

1A Ⓓ Peters Design Ⓒ Messier-Bugatti-Tracer 1B Ⓓ Moonsire Ⓒ Contract Associates
2A Ⓓ The Joe Bosack Graphic Design Co. Ⓒ ECHL 2B Ⓓ Jeff Pollard Design Ⓒ Nike
3A Ⓓ Ross Hogin Design Ⓒ Seattle Thunderbirds 3B Ⓓ Barnstorm Creative Group Inc. Ⓒ Carson Air Flight Centres

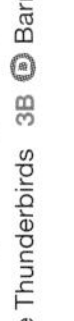

Ⓓ = Design Firm Ⓒ = Client

A | B

Ⓓ = Design Firm   Ⓒ = Client

1A Ⓓ Peterson & Company Ⓒ Eagle Materials Inc.   1B Ⓓ Walsh Associates Ⓒ Seahawk Rubber Ring Manufacturing
2A Ⓓ AKOFA Creative Ⓒ Self Promotional   2B Ⓓ Scott Oeschger Design Ⓒ Saint Joseph's Preparatory School
3A Ⓓ greteman group Ⓒ Raven Café   3B Ⓓ Sommese Design Ⓒ State College Park Preservation

1

2

3

RAVEN
CAFE

A

B

1

2

3

1A Ⓓ Typonic Ⓒ Spielerabe 1B Ⓓ Werner Design Werks Ⓒ Grand Connect
2A Ⓓ sarah watson design Ⓒ Darby James 2B Ⓓ Mohouse Design Co. Ⓒ Bright 5 Productions, LLC.
3A Ⓓ Studio Stubborn Sideburn Ⓒ Saiwai Law Firm 3B Ⓓ Cato Purnell Partners Ⓒ Hiranandani Group

Ⓓ = Design Firm Ⓒ = Client

Birds

D = Design Firm   C = Client

1A D Studio GT&P C AJ Mobilita'Srl 1B D Zwölf Sonnen C City of Bad Schwalbach
2A D ArtGraphics.ru C Stolichny Plastic 2B D Duffy & Partners C Rick Webb
3A D MINE C MINE™ 3B D Oxide Design Co. C Ommen Custom Homes

	A	B
1		
2		
3		

A

B

1

2

3

Serbian Refugee Council

1A Ⓓ Gardner Design Ⓒ New Horizon 1B Ⓓ Sabingrafik, Inc. Ⓒ Quintana
2A Ⓓ Felixsockwell.com Ⓒ dove hand 2B Ⓓ Felixsockwell.com Ⓒ NCAYV.USA
3A Ⓓ sarah watson design Ⓒ sarah watson 3B Ⓓ 38one Ⓒ SRC

Ⓓ = Design Firm Ⓒ = Client

Birds

A B

Ⓓ = Design Firm Ⓒ = Client

1A Ⓓ Chris Malven Design Ⓒ Hellfire Hot Sauce 1B Ⓓ UlrichPinciotti Design Group Ⓒ Presbyterian Villages of Michigan

2A Ⓓ Brand Navigation Ⓒ Access Knowledge 2B Ⓓ Hinge Ⓒ World Bank

3A Ⓓ Maremar Graphic Design Ⓒ Dulce Zambador 3B Ⓓ Banowetz + Company, Inc. Ⓒ Nest Egg Papers

1

2

3

	A	B
1		
2		
3		

1A Ⓓ Eben Design Ⓒ Alliance Nursing 1B Ⓓ Mohouse Design Co. Ⓒ Bright 5 Productions, LLC
2A Ⓓ Banowetz + Company, Inc. Ⓒ Nest Egg Papers 2B Ⓓ R&D thinktank Ⓒ AwakeTel
3A Ⓓ Steven O'Connor Ⓒ chicken 3B Ⓓ Gardner Design Ⓒ Backroads Traveler

Ⓓ = Design Firm Ⓒ = Client

D = Design Firm   C = Client

1A D Colle + McVoy C Ciatti's Chianti Grill 1B D ivan2design C El Pollo Loco

2A D Morse and Company Advertising Communication C Cyrano's Restaurant 2B D Element C Howe Family Reunion 2005

3A D Whence: the studio C The Krewe of Wild Turkeys 3B D KONG Design Group C Listen Skateboards

	A	B
1		
2		
3		

	A	B
1		
2		
3		

1A D Rick Johnson & Company C Quail Ranch 1B D Dashwood Design Ltd C Farrow Jamieson
2A D Sandstrom Design C White Owl 2B D Bright Strategic Design C Paradise on a Hanger
3A D Gardner Design C Bradley Paper 3B D Gardner Design C Bradley Paper

D = Design Firm C = Client

Ⓓ = Design Firm Ⓒ = Client

1A Ⓓ Fernandez Design Ⓒ Kiwi 1B Ⓓ McGuire Design Ⓒ Denise Swanson
2A Ⓓ Gardner Design Ⓒ City of Newton, KS 2B Ⓓ Doink, Inc. Ⓒ Miami Benefit Club
3A Ⓓ Michael Courtney Design, Inc. Ⓒ Maggie Martin, Midwife 3B Ⓓ Mires Ⓒ Pelican Video Games

A B

1

2

3

	A	B
1		
2	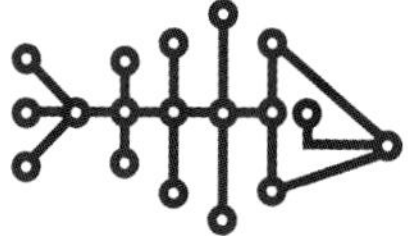	
3		

1A Ⓓ M3 Advertising Design Ⓒ Osaka Sushi 1B Ⓓ Diagram Ⓒ Aqua Park Sopot
2A Ⓓ Perfect Circle Media Group Ⓒ Tekno Sushi Bar 2B Ⓓ GSD&M Ⓒ fishdirectory.com
3A Ⓓ Fredrik Lewander Ⓒ Johan Broman 3B Ⓓ Hubbell Design Works Ⓒ Fashionfish

Ⓓ = Design Firm Ⓒ = Client

D = Design Firm C = Client

1A D Strange Ideas C Aquatic Concepts 1B D David Kampa C Blue Fish Development Group

2A D Naughtyfish C onefish twofish kidswear and maternity 2B D urbanINFLUENCE design studio C ticklefish

3A D The Logo Factory Inc. C Puff Nation Clothing 3B D Red Circle C kung fu fish

	A	B
1	AQUATIC CONCEPTS	
2	one fish two fish	
3		

	A	B
1		
2		
3		

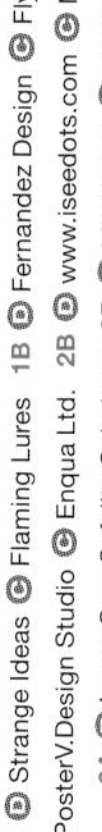

1A Ⓓ Strange Ideas Ⓒ Flaming Lures 1B Ⓓ Fernandez Design Ⓒ Flying Fish
2A Ⓓ PosterV.Design Studio Ⓒ Enqua Ltd. 2B Ⓓ www.iseedots.com Ⓒ Mike Stelzner
3A Ⓓ Lunar Cow Safelite Solutions 3B Ⓓ Mindgruve Ⓒ Cal Mar

Ⓓ = Design Firm Ⓒ = Client

Fish/Bugs/Reptiles

Ⓓ = Design Firm Ⓒ = Client

1A Ⓓ Sabingrafik, Inc. Ⓒ Chileno Bay 1B Ⓓ Sergio Bianco Ⓒ Valter Franco Ricci

2A Ⓓ Steven O'Connor Ⓒ dolphin—for sale 2B Ⓓ Peak Seven Advertising Ⓒ Waterside

3A Ⓓ Mad Dog Graphx Ⓒ Ukpeagvik Inupiat Corporation 3B Ⓓ Tom Fowler, Inc. Ⓒ The Maritime Aquarium at Norwalk

	A	B
1		
2		
3		

A

B

1

2

3

1A Ⓓ dale harris Ⓒ renega 1B Ⓓ Ammunition Ⓒ August.One Communications
2A Ⓓ The Robin Shepherd Group Ⓒ Grippers Surf Wax 2B Ⓓ FUSZION Collaborative Ⓒ The Caribbean
3A Ⓓ Glitschka Studios Ⓒ Upper Deck Company 3B Ⓓ The Robin Shepherd Group Ⓒ J. Johnson Gallery

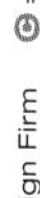

Ⓓ = Design Firm Ⓒ = Client

D = Design Firm C = Client

1A D Strange Ideas C Nautilus Pictures 1B D Cato Purnell Partners C UniSuper

2A D ZEBRA design branding C IVS Group 2B D Glitschka Studios C Upper Deck Company

3A D Cato Purnell Partners C Britz Rentals 3B D Lesniewicz Associates C China Stone

	A	B
1	 	
2	 	
3		

	A	B
1		
2		
3		

1A Ⓓ Glitschka Studios Ⓒ Upper Deck Company 1B Ⓓ Dotzero Design Ⓒ Kritis
2A Ⓓ Glitschka Studios Ⓒ Upper Deck Company 2B Ⓓ Farm Design Ⓒ Shop-o-saurus
3A Ⓓ Gardner Design Ⓒ Plastic Surgery Center 3B Ⓓ Sommese Design Ⓒ Lauth Development

Ⓓ = Design Firm Ⓒ = Client

Ⓓ = Design Firm Ⓒ = Client

1A Ⓓ Cato Purnell Partners Ⓒ beyond blue 1B Ⓓ Alphabet Arm Design Ⓒ G2G Management
2A Ⓓ Gardner Design Ⓒ Plastic Surgery Center 2B Ⓓ Brian Blankenship Ⓒ The Art Station
3A Ⓓ Tactix Creative Ⓒ Better ATM Services 3B Ⓓ Thomas Manss & Company Ⓒ Ability International

	A	B
1	 	
2		
3	 	

	A	B
1		
2		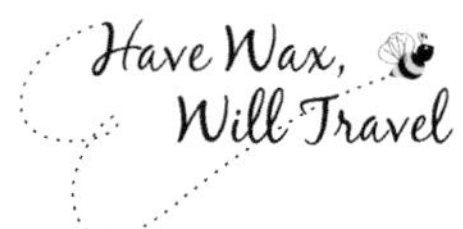
3		

1A Ⓓ Gardner Design Ⓒ Hustler 1B Ⓓ Bronson Ma Creative Ⓒ 1st American Bank
2A Ⓓ Farm Design Ⓒ Queen Bee Waxing 2B Ⓓ elf design Ⓒ Have Wax, Will Travel
3A Ⓓ Sayles Graphic Design, Inc. Ⓒ Busy Bee Tailoring 3B Ⓓ Gardner Design Ⓒ Hustler

Ⓓ = Design Firm Ⓒ = Client

D = Design Firm C = Client

1A D jsDesignCo. C buzzsaw.com 1B D Ross Hogin Design C Buzzbee
2A D Banowetz + Company, Inc. C Hotel ZaZa 2B D Banowetz + Company, Inc. C Hotel ZaZa
3A D Felixsockwell.com C firefly 3B D judson design associates C Linda and Jim Goodnight

	A	B
1		
2		Dragonfly
3	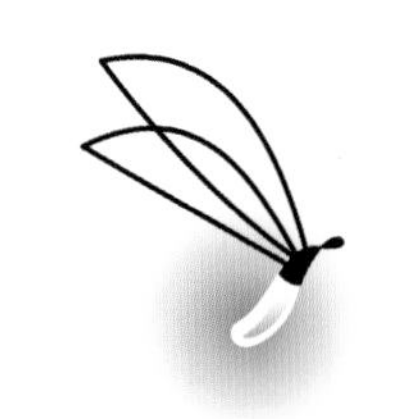	

A B

1

2

3

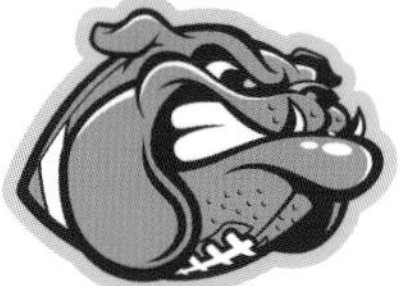

1A Ⓓ Jon Flaming Design Ⓒ Dog's Day 1B Ⓓ Elephant In The Room Ⓒ Doglogic
2A Ⓓ judson design associates Ⓒ Underdog Animation Studio 2B Ⓓ retropup Ⓒ Bowhouse
3A Ⓓ The Clockwork Group Ⓒ Bragging Rights Online 3B Ⓓ Launchpad Creative Ⓒ OKC Yard Dogs

Ⓓ = Design Firm Ⓒ = Client

Ⓓ = Design Firm Ⓒ = Client

1A Ⓓ Glitschka Studios Ⓒ Upper Deck Company 1B Ⓓ Elephant In The Room Ⓒ Doglogic

2A Ⓓ Simon & Goetz Design Ⓒ HS Fashion 2B Ⓓ DDB Dallas Ⓒ The Dog House

3A Ⓓ ROBOT Ⓒ The Palms Pet Resort and Spa 3B Ⓓ Banowetz + Company, Inc. Ⓒ Frenkel & Frenkel

	A	B
1	 	
2		
3		

	A	B
1		 
2		
3		

1A Ⓓ Blue Studios, Inc. Ⓒ Bingo Broadband 1B Ⓓ Brandia Ⓒ Galp Energia
2A Ⓓ FUSZION Collaborative Ⓒ John Guilt 2B Ⓓ Rick Johnson & company Ⓒ The Bone Bistro
3A Ⓓ Savage Design Group Ⓒ The Black Labrador 3B Ⓓ Sockeye Creative Ⓒ Lucky Labrador Brewing Company

Ⓓ = Design Firm Ⓒ = Client

	A	B
1		
2		
3		

D = Design Firm   C = Client

1A D amyHELLER design C Paws Gourmet, Inc 1B D Hausch Design Agency LLC C Jeanette Kebisek

2A D Visual Inventor Ltd. Co. C Three Legged Dog 2B D Type G C Lucky Dog Pet Boutique

3A D Insomniac Creative Studio C Hattie Larlham/Constant Companions 3B D Macnab Design Visual Communication C Animal Medical Clinic

A B

1

2

3

1A Ⓓ C. Cady Design Ⓒ Critter Sitters 1B Ⓓ Edward Allen Ⓒ Humane Society of Austin
2A Ⓓ Sommese Design Ⓒ Pet Extravaganza 2B Ⓓ NeoGine Communication Design Ltd Ⓒ Schoc Chocolatier
3A Ⓓ angryporcupine*design Ⓒ Zombiecat Productions 3B Ⓓ Diagram Ⓒ Cat Children's Clothing

(D) = Design Firm (C) = Client

1A (D) Blue Storm Design (C) ByStorm 1B (D) Eyescape (C) Liongate Capital Management
2A (D) Gardner Design (C) Material Comforts 2B (D) Gardner Design (C) Fringe Salon
3A (D) Brandia (C) Sporting Clube de Portugal 3B (D) Harwood Kirsten Leigh McCoy (C) La Casa Re

	A	B
1		
2		
3		LA CASA RE

	A	B
1		
2		
3	LONE WOLF ENERGY	

1A Ⓓ Sabet Branding Ⓒ Walid Mahmoud 1B Ⓓ Werner Design Werks Ⓒ Cheetah Valley
2A Ⓓ Honey Design Ⓒ Auburn Developments 2B Ⓓ Uhlein Design Ⓒ Fox Chase Homeowners Association
3A Ⓓ Paul Black Design Ⓒ Howard Wolf 3B Ⓓ Harkey Design Ⓒ The Wolf

Ⓓ = Design Firm Ⓒ = Client

D = Design Firm   C = Client

1A D Kinesis, Inc. C MTILDA   1B D Ikola designs... C International Species Information System

2A D R&D Thinktank C Rams   2B D Gardner Design C Hustler

3A D Campbell Fisher Design C The Phoenix Zoo   3B D Oxide Design Co. C Springbok

	A	B
1		
2		
3		

A | B

1

2

3

1A Ⓓ Bonilla Design Ⓒ Wild Game, Inc. 1B Ⓓ Deep Design Ⓒ Macauley Companies
2A Ⓓ Lesniewicz Associates Ⓒ Owens Corning 2B Ⓓ Zipper Design Ⓒ Mini Doe Boutique
3A Ⓓ Sibley Peteet Ⓒ SMAM/Hunt Realty 3B Ⓓ Sabingrafik, Inc. Ⓒ Rocky Mountain Elk Foundation

Ⓓ = Design Firm Ⓒ = Client

A | B

Ⓓ = Design Firm Ⓒ = Client

1A Ⓓ Ikola designs... Ⓒ Minnesota Zoological Society 1B Ⓓ Lesniewicz Associates Ⓒ Erie Bleu Alpaca Farm
2A Ⓓ Strategic America Ⓒ Horsepower Energy Drink 2B Ⓓ Hill Design Studios Ⓒ Red Fence Farm
3A Ⓓ Sayles Graphic Design, Inc. Ⓒ Wildwood Hills Ranch 3B Ⓓ Campbell Fisher Design Ⓒ Wildfire Golf

1

Erie Bleu
Alpaca Farm

2

3

A

B

2

1A Ⓓ Fresh Oil Ⓒ Chester's Chophouse & Wine Bar 1B Ⓓ The Joe Bosack Graphic Design Co. Ⓒ Boise State
2A Ⓓ GSCS Ⓒ Madinat Jumeirah 2B Ⓓ Hubbell Design Works Ⓒ Surf & Spa Stables
3A Ⓓ Macnab Design Visual Communication Ⓒ Maddoux-Wey Arabians 3B Ⓓ Edward Allen Ⓒ Half Moon Farm

Ⓓ = Design Firm Ⓒ = Client

D = Design Firm   C = Client

1A D Kendall Creative Shop, Inc. C Bank of America 1B D S Design, Inc. C The Coach House
2A D Whitney Edwards LLC C Biga Fund 2B D Brandia C CTT Correios
3A D UNO C Circo America 3B D Jeff Pollard Design C Hay Processing unlimited

	A	B
1	PALOMINO POINT	
2		
3		

A	B	
		1 
		2
		3

1A Ⓓ sarah watson design Ⓒ Laughing Horse Theatre 1B Ⓓ R&D Thinktank Ⓒ Nynas Strategic Design
2A Ⓓ Steven O'Connor Ⓒ Democratic Party 2B Ⓓ Howerton+White Interactive Ⓒ Buffalo Saints
3A Ⓓ Studio Simon Ⓒ Harpeth Indians 3B Ⓓ Braindig Ⓒ Bife

Ⓓ = Design Firm Ⓒ = Client

Animals

ⓓ = Design Firm   ⓒ = Client

1A ⓓ Fresh Oil ⓒ Blackstone Studios 1B ⓓ Ó! ⓒ Mjólka
2A ⓓ Banowetz + Company, Inc. ⓒ Winter Moon 2B ⓓ Brainding ⓒ AkOlzha
3A ⓓ Willoughby Design Group ⓒ Sheridan's Lattes and Frozen Custard 3B ⓓ judson design associates ⓒ Cy-Creek little league baseball team

	A	B
1		
2		
3		

A B

1

2

3

1A Ⓓ UNO Ⓒ Chile Verde 1B Ⓓ FUSZION Collaborative Ⓒ Americans for the Arts
2A Ⓓ HMK Archive Ⓒ The RK Group 2B Ⓓ Univisual Ⓒ Univisual
3A Ⓓ Studio Simon Ⓒ New Hampshire Fisher Cats 3B Ⓓ Jon Flaming Design Ⓒ Watermark Community Church ministry program

Ⓓ = Design Firm Ⓒ = Client

A | B

1

2

3

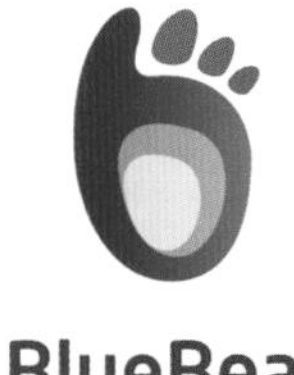

D = Design Firm C = Client

1A D Dr. Alderete C Madrid Comics store 1B D Solo Multimedia, Inc. C Great Bend Gear, ltd.

2A D ROBOT C Geostrata 2B D R&R Partners C Primm Valley Resorts

3A D Gabi Toth C Cooperativa Sociale di Orso Blu Onlus 3B D cotterteam C Conformist Skateboards

A B

1

2

3

1A Ⓓ Dr. Alderete Ⓒ Tras la Chuleta Producciones 1B Ⓓ Anoroc Ⓒ Hideaway BBQ
2A Ⓓ Gridwerk Ⓒ Two Hams Entertainment 2B Ⓓ Turner Duckworth Ⓒ Oakville Grocery
3A Ⓓ Mariqua Design Ⓒ Fauna Bath 3B Ⓓ Ross Hogin Design Ⓒ Cairo.com

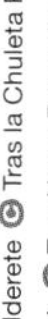
Ⓓ = Design Firm Ⓒ = Client

Animals

Ⓓ = Design Firm   Ⓒ = Client

1A Ⓓ Jon Flaming Design Ⓒ The Rock Badgers 1B Ⓓ Launchpad Creative Ⓒ Cookie Monkey

2A Ⓓ A3 Design Ⓒ Evolution Records 2B Ⓓ Creative Kong Ⓒ Creative Kong

3A Ⓓ thomas-vasquez.com Ⓒ Black Eyed Peas/A&M Records 3B Ⓓ rajasandhu.com Ⓒ Fashion Australia

	A	B
1		
2		
3		

A | B

1

2

3

1A Ⓓ Gee + Chung Design Ⓒ Imaginarium 1B Ⓓ David Kampa Ⓒ Iron Rhino
2A Ⓓ Werner Design Werks Ⓒ Indochine 2B Ⓓ 9MYLES, Inc. Ⓒ Cardamon Project
3A Ⓓ Felixsockwell.com Ⓒ gop100 3B Ⓓ Felixsockwell.com Ⓒ gop100

Ⓓ = Design Firm Ⓒ = Client

D = Design Firm   C = Client

1A D Boelts/Stratford Associates C Zoo Logo 1B D Gardner Design C StackShack

2A D Campbell Fisher Design C The Phoenix Zoo 2B D Eyebeam Creative LLC C World Wildlife Fund

3A D The Clockwork Group C San Antonio Zoo 3B D Matt Whitley C Cabela's

	A	B
1		
2		
3		

A | B

1

2

3

1A (D) Gardner Design (C) Wichita Recreation & Park 1B (D) Strange Ideas (C) Recycle Mind
2A (D) Intersection Creative (C) Geno's Landscape Maintenance 2B (D) Enterprise IG (C) Tsb
3A (D) NeoGine Communication Design Ltd (C) Cerno Ltd 3B (D) Franke + Fiorella (C) Cargill

(D) = Design Firm (C) = Client

D = Design Firm   C = Client

1A D o2 ideas C SAGE Restaurant 1B D Zapata Design C Finewood Landscaping
2A D www.iseedots.com C Brinkley Design 2B D Brand Engine C Mighty Leaf Tea Company
3A D Metroparks of the Toledo Area C Metroparks of the Toledo Area 3B D Boelts/Stratford Associates C Acid Rain

	A	B
1		
2		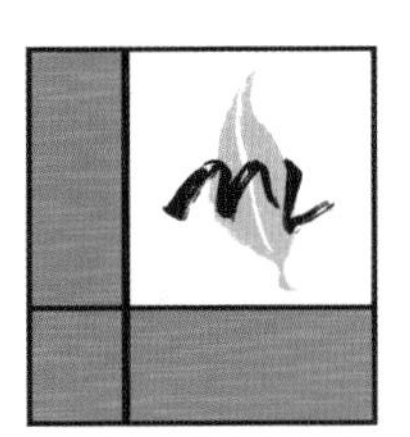

A

B

1

KINGSTON SCULPTURE BIENNIAL 2005

2

Sandalo

3

BOISE

1A Ⓓ Zapata Design Ⓒ Pines Montessori School 1B Ⓓ Ditto! Ⓒ Arts Society of Kingston
2A Ⓓ Tactix Creative Ⓒ Meritage Corp. 2B Ⓓ Braue; Branding & Corporate Design Ⓒ van der Linden
3A Ⓓ greteman group Ⓒ Boise Center 3B Ⓓ Addison Whitney Ⓒ Banner Parmacaps

Ⓓ = Design Firm Ⓒ = Client

A | B

1

essentials
MIND BODY & SOUL

2

TODD A. FRANKLIN, D.D.S.

3

D = Design Firm C = Client

1A D UlrichPinciotti Design Group C Otsego Schools 1B D Polkadot C Advanced Clinical Systems
2A D octane inc. C Renewable Energy Resources 2B D Monster Design Company C Todd A. Franklin, D.D.S.
3A D Design One C Vraiterre 3B D Octavo Designs C Old Town Tea Co.

A | B

1

2

3

1A Ⓓ Visual Inventor Ltd. Co. Ⓒ Leigh Howell Love 1B Ⓓ ginger griffin marketing and design Ⓒ The Enrichment Project

2A Ⓓ Peterson & Company Ⓒ sage theatre group 2B Ⓓ CAPSULE Ⓒ Prairie Stone Pharmacy

3A Ⓓ Freshwater Design Ⓒ North Hills 3B Ⓓ Glitschka Studios Ⓒ Cardwell Creative

Ⓓ = Design Firm Ⓒ = Client

A | B

Ⓓ = Design Firm Ⓒ = Client

1A Ⓓ Cato Purnell Partners Ⓒ IDP 1B Ⓓ GrafiQa Graphic Design Ⓒ NYSHA
2A Ⓓ KOESTER design Ⓒ TobaccoCafe.com 2B Ⓓ INNFUSION Studios Ⓒ Agave Films
3A Ⓓ Modern Dog Design Co. Ⓒ Newport Corporate 3B Ⓓ Glitschka Studios Ⓒ Macore Company

1

2

3

A

B

1

2

3

1A D Chimera Design C Svarmisk 1B D IMAGEHAUS C Twin Oaks Marine
2A D Carol Gravelle Graphic Design C Tournesol Siteworks 2B D Strange Ideas C Kansas Stars
3A D Diagram C ING Real Estate Development 3B D Anoroc C Bubel Aiken Foundation

D = Design Firm C = Client

D = Design Firm C = Client

1A D Mattson Creative C Centex Homes 1B D juls design inc C The Iowa Clinic
2A D Shawn Hazen Graphic Design C Self 2B D Sterling Brands C America Online
3A D Cato Purnell Partners C Flower Factory 3B D ROBOT C SunJoi Corporation

	A	B
1		
2		
3		

A

B

1

2

3

1A Ⓓ Armeilia Subianto Design Ⓒ Nuansa Asri Cipadu 1B Ⓓ Boom Creative Ⓒ Neighborhood Lawn Care
2A Ⓓ Bright Strategic Design Ⓒ Daily Colors 2B Ⓓ Strange Ideas Ⓒ Botania
3A Ⓓ B.L.A. Design Company Ⓒ NABC 3B Ⓓ Gardner Design Ⓒ Material Comforts

Ⓓ = Design Firm Ⓒ = Client

A B

1

INN AT BEVERLY HILLS

2

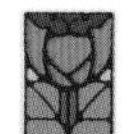

PROSPECT PLACE
apartments

3

POPPYSEED CAKE
INVITATIONS · CARDS

FRANCE JACMAIN
STYLIST

Ⓓ = Design Firm Ⓒ = Client

1A Ⓓ Banowetz + Company, Inc., Ⓒ Inn at Beverly Hills 1B Ⓓ Zombie Design Ⓒ Corham Company
2A Ⓓ octane inc. Ⓒ JB Communications 2B Ⓓ Sergio Bianco Ⓒ Pico Maccario
3A Ⓓ elf design Ⓒ Poppyseed Cake 3B Ⓓ Ardoise Design Ⓒ Immotik inc.

A | B

1

2

3

1A Ⓓ GetElevatedDesign.com Ⓒ Green Lotus Grounds 1B Ⓓ Lisa Starace Ⓒ jardín
2A Ⓓ baba designs Ⓒ Enchanted Minstrel Music 2B Ⓓ The Pink Pear Design Company Ⓒ Idlewild Jewelry Design
3A Ⓓ Mattson Creative Ⓒ Shea Homes 3B Ⓓ design-studio Muhina Ⓒ Karakulino Milk

D = Design Firm C = Client

1A D seed C seed 1B D Brandient C GlaxoSmithKline

2A D Imaginaria C Azteca Milling 2B D HMK Archive C euroCatalyst

3A D Rickabaugh Graphics C Mountain View Coffee Roasters 3B D Methodologie C Gourmondo Catering

A

B

1

2

3

	A	B
1		
2		
3		

1A Ⓓ Zwölf Sonnen Ⓒ Förderverein Fachhochschule Wiesbaden 1B Ⓓ Brand Navigation Ⓒ Conifer Specialties
2A Ⓓ Gardner Design Ⓒ The Lone Ranger 2B Ⓓ The Flores Shop Ⓒ The Cedarhouse School
3A Ⓓ Richards Brock Miller Mitchell & Associates Ⓒ The Home Depot 3B Ⓓ Curtis Sharp Design Ⓒ Asah Terra

Ⓓ = Design Firm Ⓒ = Client

A B

1

2

3

Ⓓ = Design Firm Ⓒ = Client

1A Ⓓ OmniStudio Inc Ⓒ Modern Africa 1B Ⓓ Ramp Ⓒ compLife
2A Ⓓ Hinge Ⓒ Bonsai Labs 2B Ⓓ Miriello Grafico, Inc. Ⓒ Barratt American
3A Ⓓ Mohouse Design Co. Ⓒ Lakewood Service League 3B Ⓓ Actual Size Creative Ⓒ Shady Grove

A

B

1

2

ORCHARD GROUP

3

1A Ⓓ Napoleon design Ⓒ APAE—Associação de Pais e Amigos dos Excepcionais—Bauru 1B Ⓓ Sibley Peteet Ⓒ Sanders\Wingo
2A Ⓓ www.iseedots.com Ⓒ Orchard Group, Inc. 2B Ⓓ The Collaboration Ⓒ City of Glendale
3A Ⓓ The Robin Shepherd Group Ⓒ Earth Day 3B Ⓓ Diagram Ⓒ Plantec

Ⓓ = Design Firm Ⓒ = Client

D = Design Firm   C = Client

1A D Felixsockwell.com C Cigna 1B D Simon & Goetz Design C Elenxis

2A D Brandia C BancoBIC 2B D christiansen : creative C liveliberal.org

3A D joe miller's company C Shade 3B D the zen kitchen C Branches Fine Gifts

	A	B
1		
2		
3		

	A	B
1		
2		
3		

1A Ⓓ concussion, llc Ⓒ Treehouse Foods, Inc. 1B Ⓓ judson design associates Ⓒ Chinquapin School
2A Ⓓ Mires Ⓒ Harmonium 2B Ⓓ Gardner Design Ⓒ The Chapel
3A Ⓓ Phillips Design Ⓒ Oregon Potato Commission/Pihas, Schmidt & Westerdahl 3B Ⓓ Wells Fargo Financial Ⓒ Wells Fargo Financial

Ⓓ = Design Firm Ⓒ = Client

A B

D = Design Firm C = Client

1A D Squires & Company C City of Arlington, TX 1B D David Kampa C Live Oak Brewing Company
2A D Studio GT&P C Artigianato Umbro Srl 2B D Steven O'Connor C Palm Coast Security
3A D Visual Moxie C Huez Venetian Plaster 3B D Dreamedia Studios C Cyprus Village

1

2

3

A

B

1

2

3

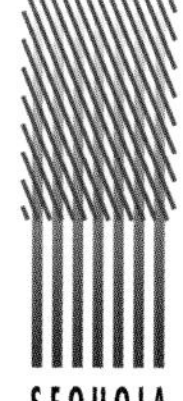

1A Ⓓ Gardner Design Ⓒ The Chapel 1B Ⓓ GingerBee Creative Ⓒ Bozeman Arbor Care
2A Ⓓ Visual Inventory Ltd. Co. Ⓒ Hentges Tree Service 2B Ⓓ KOESTER design Ⓒ Mobil Land Development
3A Ⓓ tanagram partners Ⓒ Triple Tree Capital 3B Ⓓ REINES DESIGN INC. Ⓒ SEQUOIA

Ⓓ = Design Firm Ⓒ = Client

	A	B
1		CHINA SKY
2		
3		

D = Design Firm   C = Client

1A D dale harris C Quambatook Retirement Village Management 1B D Fresh Oil C China Sky
2A D Sabingrafik, Inc. C Amore 2B D Pixelspace C Glass Roots Studio
3A D Design and Image C RedCloud Capital 3B D Propeller C Dubai Executive Office

A | B

1

Skyscraper

VENTURES

2

zen

solutions

3

1A Ⓓ Glitschka Studios Ⓒ Green Living Magazine 1B Ⓓ Kitemath Ⓒ Skyscraper Ventures
2A Ⓓ Harkey Design Ⓒ Zen Solutions 2B Ⓓ Werner Design Werks Ⓒ Aether for Nike
3A Ⓓ Kitemath Ⓒ First Geneva 3B Ⓓ McAndrew Kaps Ⓒ One Source Wealth Management

Ⓓ = Design Firm Ⓒ = Client

Nature

Ⓓ = Design Firm Ⓒ = Client

1A Ⓓ Lippincott Mercer Ⓒ RiverSource 1B Ⓓ Hanna & Associates Ⓒ Hayden Homes
2A Ⓓ Cato Purnell Partners Ⓒ BenQ 2B Ⓓ greteman group Ⓒ connect west. fin
3A Ⓓ Lulu Strategy Ⓒ Lillian Montalto Signature Properties 3B Ⓓ Glitschka Studios Ⓒ Ralston 360

	A	B
1	RiverSource	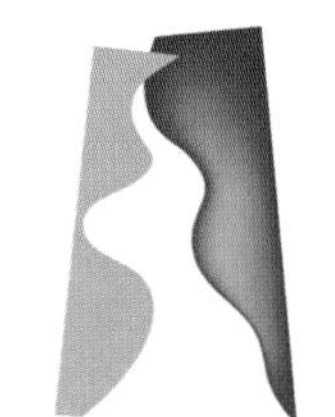
2		
3		

A | B

1

2

3

1A Ⓓ UNO Ⓒ Mercado Central 1B Ⓓ Brandia Ⓒ Eco Loja
2A Ⓓ Funk/Levis & Associates, Inc. Ⓒ University of Oregon Summer School 2B Ⓓ greteman group Ⓒ moon fire
3A Ⓓ Mattson Creative Ⓒ Scott Jeffrey 3B Ⓓ R&R Partners Ⓒ Insomnia Entertainment

Ⓓ = Design Firm Ⓒ = Client

	A	B
1	ASSURANT	
2		
3		

D = Design Firm   C = Client

1A D Carbone Smolan Agency C Assurant   1B D Cato Purnell Partners C Bank Direct
2A D David Kampa C David Carter Design   2B D Gee + Chung Design C Sun Microsystems
3A D Brainding C grupo H   3B D Gardner Design C X-Cursion

	A	B
1		
2		
3		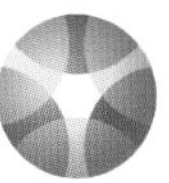

1A Ⓓ Strategy Studio Ⓒ International Resource Center 1B Ⓓ R&R Partners Ⓒ Airwave
2A Ⓓ Fernandez Design Ⓒ Citrix 2B Ⓓ Brandia Ⓒ Sporting Clube de Portugal
3A Ⓓ switchfoot creative Ⓒ Conquest Trading Co. 3B Ⓓ Landor Associates Ⓒ Centigon

Ⓓ = Design Firm Ⓒ = Client

D = Design Firm C = Client

1A D switchfoot creative C Xcelcius 1B D Cato Purnell Partners C Terry White Chemists

2A D Strange Ideas C Oceania 2B D Brandia C INAS FID

3A D Thomas Manss & Company C VCC Perfect Pictures 3B D Shift design C SDNM

	A	B
1		TerryWhite chemists
2	 OCEANIA	 4° INAS-FID Campeonato de Futebol EURO'03
3	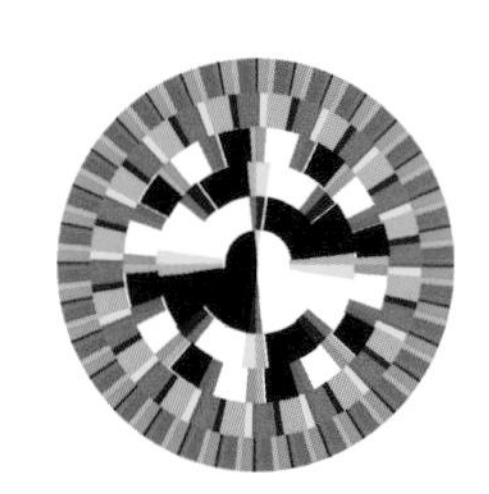	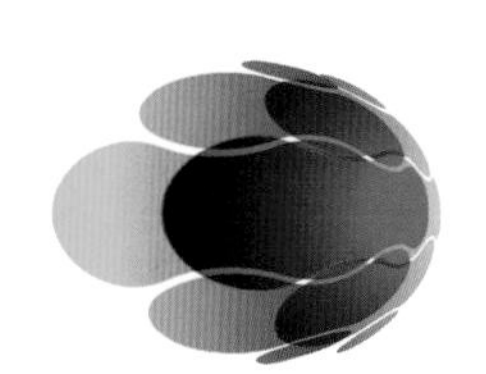

	A	B
1		
2		
3		

1A Ⓓ tanagram partners Ⓒ Davidson Oil 1B Ⓓ Sterling Brands Ⓒ Cablevision
2A Ⓓ Gee Creative Ⓒ Turnkey Technology Solutions 2B Ⓓ Mindspace Ⓒ Omnilink Systems
3A Ⓓ www.iseedots.com Ⓒ Snackmoney Records 3B Ⓓ Joi Design Ⓒ Simple Software Training

Ⓓ = Design Firm Ⓒ = Client

Ⓓ = Design Firm Ⓒ = Client

1A Ⓓ dale harris Ⓒ full bled circle symbol 1B Ⓓ Dialekt Design Ⓒ Tapspace Publications

2A Ⓓ Fox Parlor Ⓒ Lita Reyes 2B Ⓓ Barnstorm Creative Ⓒ Equity Momentum

3A Ⓓ Land Design Ⓒ Pulte Homes, Inc. 3B Ⓓ Paragon Design International Ⓒ Chicago Harbors

	A	B
1		
2		
3		

A | B

1

2

3

1A Ⓓ Brandia Ⓒ Ola 1B Ⓓ Brandia Ⓒ Galp Energia
2A Ⓓ Dashwood Design Ltd Ⓒ Unison 2B Ⓓ Ross Hogin Design Ⓒ Paragon Media
3A Ⓓ Ikola designs... Ⓒ Sunstar Foods 3B Ⓓ BLOOM LLC Ⓒ BLOOM

Ⓓ = Design Firm Ⓒ = Client

A B

Ⓓ = Design Firm Ⓒ = Client

1A Ⓓ Gardner Design Ⓒ New Horizon 1B Ⓓ Living Creative Design Ⓒ San José State University
2A Ⓓ Brainding Ⓒ Ideal Exposure 2B Ⓓ mattisimo Ⓒ coastal surfwear
3A Ⓓ Brand Bird Ⓒ Arby's 3B Ⓓ mattisimo Ⓒ pod interior design

1

2

3

A

B

1

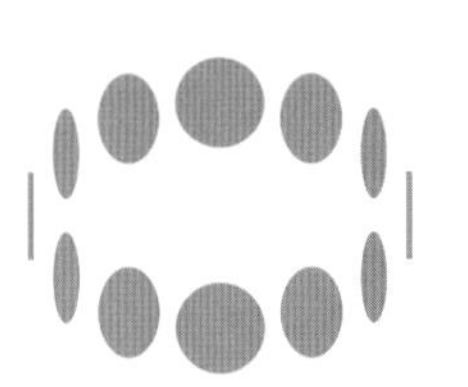

2

3

1A Ⓓ Starlight Studio Ⓒ RM Custom Creations 1B Ⓓ Gee + Chung Design Ⓒ Art Center College of Design
2A Ⓓ Joi Design Ⓒ Cluster Consulting Group 2B Ⓓ tanagram partners Ⓒ Darc Corporation
3A Ⓓ Sutter Design Ⓒ Quest 3B Ⓓ reduced fat Ⓒ John Zack

Ⓓ = Design Firm Ⓒ = Client

	A	B
1		ProteoPlex™
2	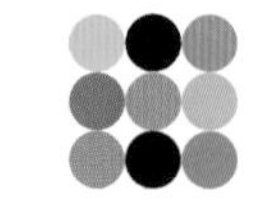 HYATT PLACE	
3		

D = Design Firm   C = Client

1A D Q C tks solutions 1B D Justin Johnson C ProteoPlex

2A D Lippincott Mercer C Hyatt Place 2B D FUSZION Collaborative C FUSZION Collaborative

3A D Ross Hogin Design C Connetics MMG 3B D Bronson Ma Creative C Parago, Inc.

A | B

1

2

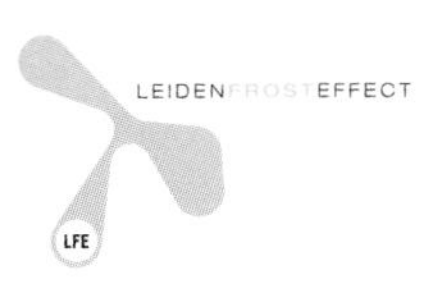

3

plusinfinite

mediaengine

1A Ⓓ d4 creative group Ⓒ Ethidium 1B Ⓓ Glitschka Studios Ⓒ Cyphon Design
2A Ⓓ A3 Design Ⓒ LFE 2B Ⓓ Brainding Ⓒ bump networks
3A Ⓓ Brainding Ⓒ PlusInfinite 3B Ⓓ Grapefruit Ⓒ Media Engine LLC

Ⓓ = Design Firm Ⓒ = Client

D = Design Firm   C = Client

1A D Interrobang Design Collaborative, Inc. C Internal Monologue   1B D elaine park C Akina Inc.
2A D bunch C Listen in—Portugal   2B D Kaimere C Goosebumps Records
3A D tanagram partners C Valence Health   3B D Kym Abrams Design C Montgomery Ward/Mobil

	A	B
1	InternalMonologue	
2		
3		

A | B

1

2

cognistar

3

1A Ⓓ Gee + Chung Design Ⓒ Netigy Corporation 1B Ⓓ A3 Design Ⓒ New Jack Soul
2A Ⓓ Lippincott Mercer Ⓒ Cognistar 2B Ⓓ Gardner Design Ⓒ Spirit Aerosystems 8
3A Ⓓ FutureBrand Ⓒ Buenos Aires Province Government 3B Ⓓ FutureBrand Ⓒ Tractebel Peru

Ⓓ = Design Firm Ⓒ = Client

Ⓓ = Design Firm Ⓒ = Client

1A Ⓓ Brian Blankenship Ⓒ Jetta 1B Ⓓ Steven O'Connor Ⓒ Nowiejski 401(k) Associates, LP

2A Ⓓ Braue; Branding & Corporate Design Ⓒ Concore 2B Ⓓ Maremar Graphic Design Ⓒ Abbott Laboratories

3A Ⓓ Letter 7 Ⓒ SixPointStudios 3B Ⓓ Axiom Design Partners Ⓒ STAR Peer Tutoring Programme

	A	B
1	 	
2		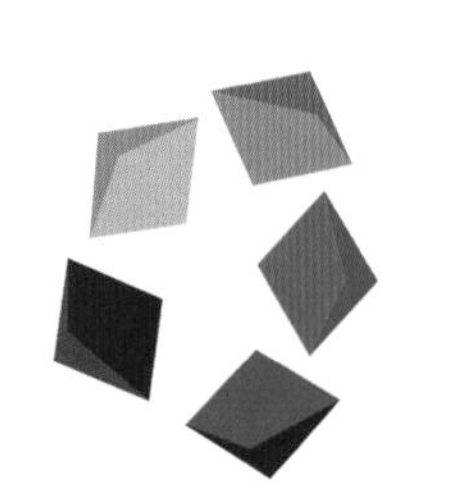
3		

	A	B
1		
2		
3		

1A Ⓓ Gardner Design Ⓒ VizWorx 1B Ⓓ Unibrand Belgrade Ⓒ pink film
2A Ⓓ Steven O'Connor Ⓒ EZLN 2B Ⓓ S Design, Inc. Ⓒ Thinking Cap/Oklahoma Partnership for School Readiness
3A Ⓓ Gabriela Gasparini Design Ⓒ Miracle Mind 3B Ⓓ thomas-vasquez.com Ⓒ Book Forum—Frankfurt, Germany

Ⓓ = Design Firm Ⓒ = Client

Ⓓ = Design Firm Ⓒ = Client

1A Ⓓ Brand Navigation Ⓒ City Bible Church 1B Ⓓ Eisenberg And Associates Ⓒ Systemware
2A Ⓓ Unibrand Belgrade Ⓒ Naftagas 2B Ⓓ Brandia Ⓒ Camara Municipal de Oeiras
3A Ⓓ Dirty Design Ⓒ Optimum Mastering 3B Ⓓ Eisenberg and Associates Ⓒ Systemware

	A	B
1	PortlandBibleCollege	
2		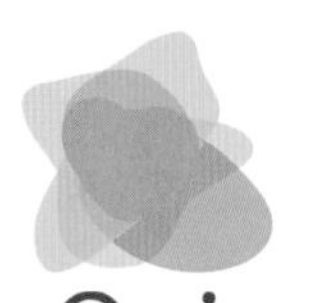
3		

	A	B
1		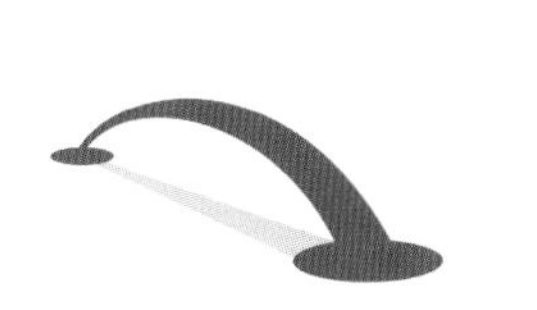
2		
3		

1A (D) Diagram (C) ING Real Estate Development 1B (D) Mindspace (C) Destinator Technologies

2A (D) Dan Rood Design (C) China Pathway Logistics 2B (D) Cato Purnell Partners (C) Guangzhou Baiyun International Airport

3A (D) Carbone Smolan Agency (C) Brooklyn Botanic Garden 3B (D) Lippincott Mercer (C) First Citizens Bank

(D) = Design Firm (C) = Client

A B

1

2

3

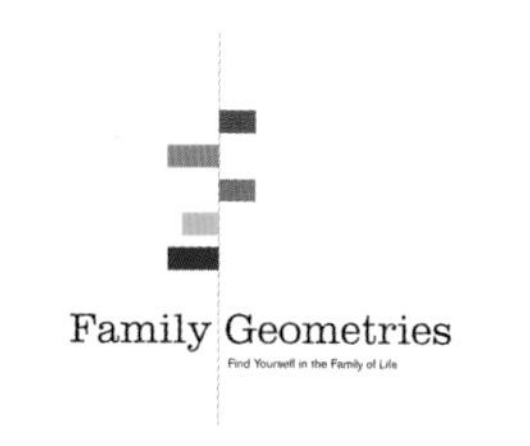

Ⓓ = Design Firm Ⓒ = Client

1A Ⓓ Brandient Ⓒ Romanian National Radio Communications Society SA 1B Ⓓ Onoma, LLC Ⓒ Diversity Initiative Group for LeBoeuf, Lam, Green & MacRae LLP

2A Ⓓ Cato Purnell Partners Ⓒ Infratil 2B Ⓓ Polemic Design Ⓒ Sophistication by Roseanne Bianchetta

3A Ⓓ MANMADE Ⓒ Family Geometries 3B Ⓓ Thomas Manss & Company Ⓒ Oberhavel Holding

	A	B
1	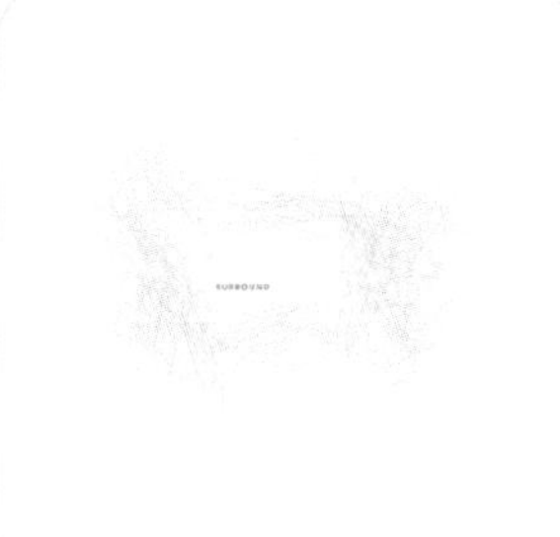	
2		
3		

1A Ⓓ Sandstrom Design Ⓒ Surround Architects 1B Ⓓ Kendall Ross Ⓒ Precept Brands
2A Ⓓ Imaginaria Ⓒ IPQ Networks 2B Ⓓ NeoGine Communication Design Ltd Ⓒ Paragee
3A Ⓓ Device Ⓒ Book Logo 1 3B Ⓓ Cheri Gearhart, graphic design Ⓒ Sarah's Inn

Ⓓ = Design Firm Ⓒ = Client

Ⓓ = Design Firm Ⓒ = Client

1A Ⓓ Polemic Design Ⓒ Proposal 1B Ⓓ Jeff Pollard Design Ⓒ Cornish College of the Arts

2A Ⓓ Lippincott Mercer Ⓒ The Bank of New York 2B Ⓓ Cato Purnell Partners Ⓒ Clearview

3A Ⓓ Kineto Ⓒ PT Karya Deka Pancamurni 3B Ⓓ Gardner Design Ⓒ The Chapel

	A	B
1		
2	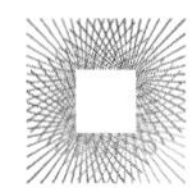 The BANK of NEW YORK	
3	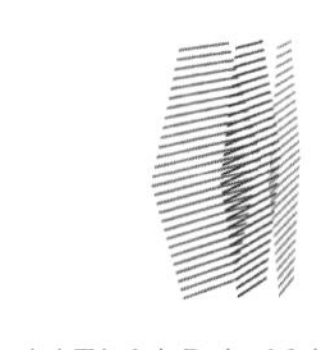 	

A

B

1

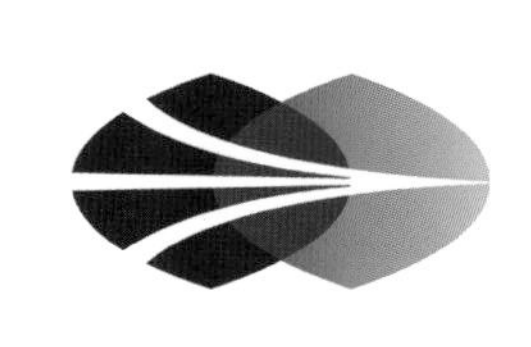

2

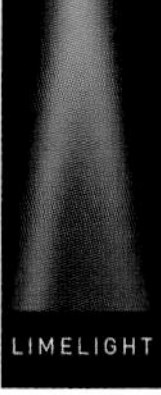

3

1A Ⓓ Brandia Ⓒ Radio Televisão Portuguesa 1B Ⓓ 28 LIMITED BRAND Ⓒ Schleupen AG
2A Ⓓ Gardner Design Ⓒ Spirit Aerosystems 2B Ⓓ Visual coolness Ⓒ Experience Analysts International
3A Ⓓ Gardner Design Ⓒ Spirit Aerosystems 3B Ⓓ Dashwood Design Ltd Ⓒ The EDGE

Ⓓ = Design Firm Ⓒ = Client

A B

1

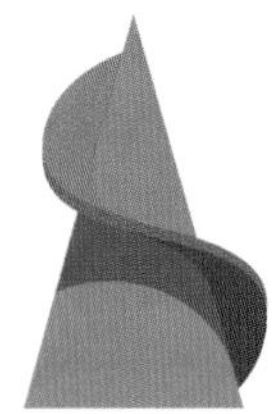

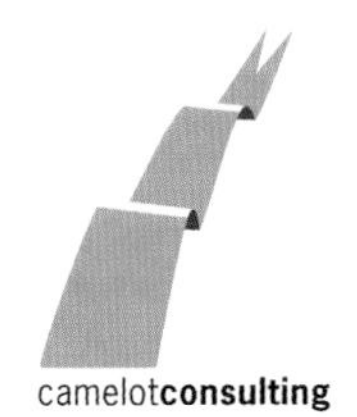

2

3

Ⓓ = Design Firm Ⓒ = Client

1A Ⓓ Mirko Ilić Corp Ⓒ Broadmoor Engineering 1B Ⓓ Barnstorm Creative Ⓒ Camelot Consulting

2A Ⓓ FutureBrand Ⓒ InBest Forex 2B Ⓓ Grapefruit Ⓒ UCS Romania

3A Ⓓ Braue; Branding & Corporate Design Ⓒ Thomas Marine Consultants 3B Ⓓ Velocity Design Works Ⓒ Pixelalbum

A

B

1

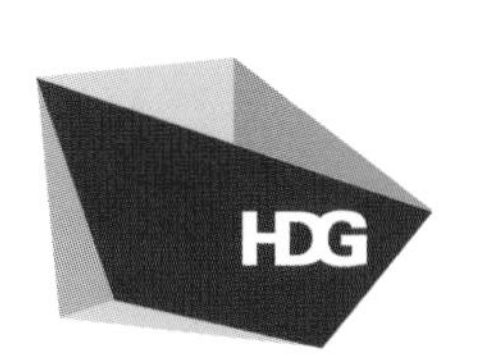

2

3

1A Ⓓ Onoma, LLC Ⓒ New York Terminals 1B Ⓓ Hutchinson Associates, Inc. Ⓒ Hutchinson Design Group
2A Ⓓ judson design associates Ⓒ Unused 2B Ⓓ CS Design Ⓒ xTech
3A Ⓓ 28 LIMITED BRAND Ⓒ Ulrich Volwinkel 3B Ⓓ Octane Ⓒ Alliance Commercial Real Estate

Ⓓ = Design Firm Ⓒ = Client

	A	B
1	propello	
2	DeVry 	
3		

D = Design Firm   C = Client

1A D Brand Engine C Propello 1B D Aurora Design C Mohawk Paper Mills
2A D Lippincott Mercer C DeVry 2B D FutureBrand C HSBC Argentina
3A D Dashwood Design Ltd C Fonterra 3B D KW43 BRANDDESIGN C Mannesmann Plastics Machinery

	A	B
1		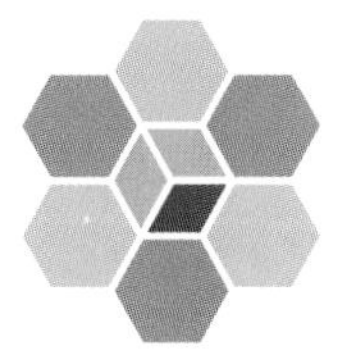
2		 sevierHeights
3		 GRAND PARK HOTEL

1A Ⓓ Sabet Branding Ⓒ Exagon 1B Ⓓ Letter 7 Ⓒ B2B Shipping Network
2A Ⓓ Shawn Hazen Graphic Design Ⓒ Bonk 2B Ⓓ Designsensory Ⓒ Sevier Heights Baptist Church
3A Ⓓ Glitschka Studios Ⓒ Ralston 360 3B Ⓓ Design MG Ⓒ for sale

Ⓓ = Design Firm Ⓒ = Client

Ⓓ = Design Firm   Ⓒ = Client

1A Ⓓ o2 ideas Ⓒ Crave Chocolatier 1B Ⓓ UltraVirgo Creative Ⓒ Polyamorous NYC
2A Ⓓ josh higgins design Ⓒ San Diego City College 2B Ⓓ Alphabet Arm Design Ⓒ Amanda Palmer
3A Ⓓ batesneimand Ⓒ The Fund for Animals 3B Ⓓ Sabingrafik, Inc. Ⓒ Trinchero Family Estates

A | B

1

2

3

	A	B
1		
2		
3		

1A Ⓓ R&R Partners Ⓒ New Vistas 1B Ⓓ A3 Design Ⓒ Dubois County Humane Society
2A Ⓓ Strategy Studio Ⓒ Christine's Fine Bake Goods 2B Ⓓ Howerton + White Interactive Ⓒ hart_1
3A Ⓓ Brainding Ⓒ Sante Coffee 3B Ⓓ Tactix Creative Ⓒ Invictus Group

Ⓓ = Design Firm Ⓒ = Client

D = Design Firm   C = Client

1A D Bryan Cooper Design C American Heart Association 1B D Rome & Gold Creative C Amigo Fiel

2A D Straka Dusan C ProSiebenSat.1 Production 2B D Straka Dusan C proposal

3A D ArtGraphics,ru C Aqua Vision 3B D UNO S Su-Frida

	A	B
1		
2		
3		

A

B

1

2

3

1A D Insight Design C My Volunteer Center 1B D Brainding C Colliervielle
2A D octane inc. C Ultra Design 2B D urbanINFLUENCE design studio C Torrid Romance Publishers
3A D Gardner Design C Big Dog Motorcycles 3B D Bronson Ma Creative C 63 Ministry

D = Design Firm C = Client

A B

1

2

3

Ⓓ = Design Firm Ⓒ = Client

1A Ⓓ Howling Good Designs Ⓒ headline communications 1B Ⓓ Gardner Design Ⓒ Ballet Wichita
2A Ⓓ Day Six Creative Ⓒ Eternal Oil & Gas 2B Ⓓ Chris Malven Design Ⓒ WestStreet Deli
3A Ⓓ Steven O'Connor Ⓒ open 3B Ⓓ Fox Parlor Ⓒ Parahamsa

A | B

1

2

FIREHOUSE
LOUNGE

3

1A Ⓓ Les Kerr Creative Ⓒ Trailblazer Studios 1B Ⓓ Parachute Design Ⓒ Sansei, Inc.
2A Ⓓ Metroparks of the Toledo Area Ⓒ Metroparks of the Toledo Area 2B Ⓓ Actual Size Creative Ⓒ Firehouse Lounge
3A Ⓓ A3 Design Ⓒ Hot Sake 3B Ⓓ Big Bald Guy Design Studio Ⓒ Benet Heating and Brazing

Ⓓ = Design Firm Ⓒ = Client

D = Design Firm   C = Client

1A D Fuego3 C Fuego3 1B D Curtis Sayers Design C The MathWorks
2A D Gabi Toth C Jester (UK) Limited 2B D Ditto! C Books for Boys
3A D Diagram C Swoboda Telecommunications 3B D Lienhart Design C Illinois Summer School for the Arts

	A	B
1		
2		
3		

A | B

1

2

3

1A Ⓓ Paul Black Design Ⓒ AquaStar Pools 1B Ⓓ Gardner Design Ⓒ Spectrum
2A Ⓓ GSD&M Ⓒ Texas Aerospace Consortium 2B Ⓓ INNFUSION Studios Ⓒ INNFUSION Studios
3A Ⓓ Sandstrom Design Ⓒ Converse 3B Ⓓ concussion, llc Ⓒ Texas Alliance of Dentists

Ⓓ = Design Firm Ⓒ = Client

A | B

D = Design Firm C = Client

1A D Mindspace C Armorworks 1B D switchfoot creative C Beach Hunter
2A D Gee + Chung Design C Sun Microsystems 2B D Jeff Pollard Design C Nike
3A D REINES DESIGN INC. C CONEKTA 3B D Fifth Letter C Enviro-Air Solutions

3

A | B

1

2

3

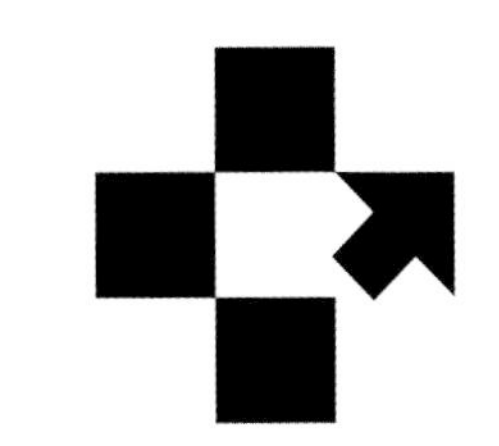

1A Ⓓ Cato Purnell Partners Ⓒ City Rail 1B Ⓓ MEME ENGINE Ⓒ PROJECT MOVEMENT
2A Ⓓ Glitschka Studios Ⓒ IMB—Fresh ID 2B Ⓓ Brandia Ⓒ GroundForce
3A Ⓓ Lesniewicz Associates Ⓒ Medical Office Solutions 3B Ⓓ Jeff Pollard Design Ⓒ wiredMD

Ⓓ = Design Firm Ⓒ = Client

Ⓓ = Design Firm   Ⓒ = Client

1A Ⓓ Diagram Ⓒ BSR   1B Ⓓ Gardner Design Ⓒ New Horizon

2A Ⓓ Gardner Design Ⓒ New Horizon   2B Ⓓ Flaxenfield, Inc. Ⓒ Traingle AIDS Interfaith Network

3A Ⓓ Mindspace Ⓒ Central Christian Church   3B Ⓓ Born to Design Ⓒ Tabernacle Presbyterian Church for : Fishhook

	A	B
1		
2		
3		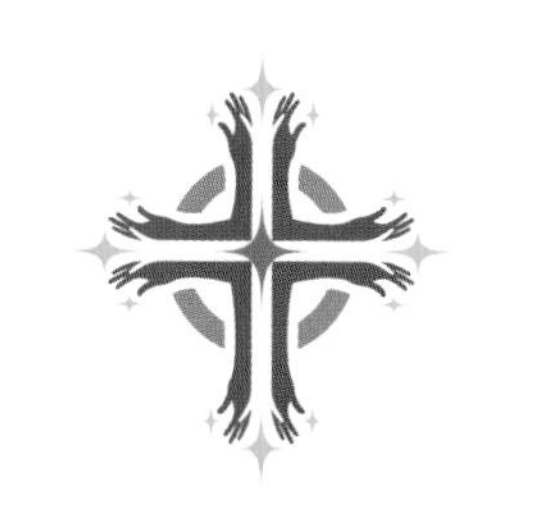

	A	B
1		
2		
3		

1A Ⓓ Exti Dzyn Ⓒ Peter & John Radio Fellowship 1B Ⓓ The Oesterle Ⓒ Edition 52
2A Ⓓ Hoyne Design Ⓒ Bolinda Publishing 2B Ⓓ R&R Partners Ⓒ Clark County School District
3A Ⓓ Lesniewicz Associates Ⓒ Toledo Museum of Art 3B Ⓓ Paul Black Design Ⓒ Stevenson Printing

Ⓓ = Design Firm Ⓒ = Client

Ⓓ = Design Firm Ⓒ = Client

1A Ⓓ thomas-vasquez.com Ⓒ book parade 1B Ⓓ Shelley Design + Marketing Ⓒ Donald Carstens
2A Ⓓ Kitemath Ⓒ J. Noelle 2B Ⓓ Brook Group, LTD Ⓒ 9 Stories High
3A Ⓓ Hornall Anderson Ⓒ BLRB Architects 3B Ⓓ David Kampa Ⓒ Texas Book Festival

	A	B
1		
2		
3		

A

B

1

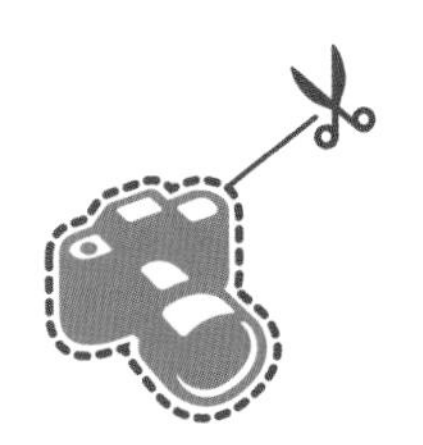

2

3

1A Ⓓ Chimera Design Ⓒ Smart Shots 1B Ⓓ The Oesterle Ⓒ Freisteller
2A Ⓓ zengigi design Ⓒ Christina Maxwell 2B Ⓓ CONCEPTiCONS Ⓒ Lorin Crosby
3A Ⓓ Hallmark Cards Inc. Ⓒ Hallmark Cards, Inc. 3B Ⓓ Idle Hands Design Ⓒ Short End Productions, LLC

Ⓓ = Design Firm Ⓒ = Client

A B

1

picturebrains

laughing stock

2

3

Ⓓ = Design Firm Ⓒ = Client

1A Ⓓ o2 ideas Ⓒ Picture Brains 1B Ⓓ Steve's Portfolio Ⓒ Laughing Stock
2A Ⓓ Straka Dusan Ⓒ Stiphout 2B Ⓓ ykcreative, LLC Ⓒ Chris Kelly
3A Ⓓ Edward Allen Ⓒ Dennis Fagan 3B Ⓓ The Oesterle Ⓒ Christoph Kappl

A

B

1

2

3

1A Ⓓ The Oesterle Ⓒ Cinema 1B Ⓓ Culture A.D. Ⓒ Independent Black Film Festival
2A Ⓓ Jonathan Rice & Company Ⓒ RadioShack 2B Ⓓ Creative Kong Ⓒ Organic Films
3A Ⓓ Werner Design Werks Ⓒ TvbyGirls 3B Ⓓ Werner Design Werks Ⓒ TVbyGirls

Ⓓ = Design Firm Ⓒ = Client

D = Design Firm   C = Client

1A D Les Kerr Creative C The Station Store 1B D Rome & Gold Creative C World-View Café
2A D Fernandez Design C Citrix 2B D The Oesterle C Micro Consult
3A D Glitschka Studios C Glitschka Studios 3B D HMK Archive C NPR KSTX

	A	B
1		
2		
3		

	A	B
1 		
2	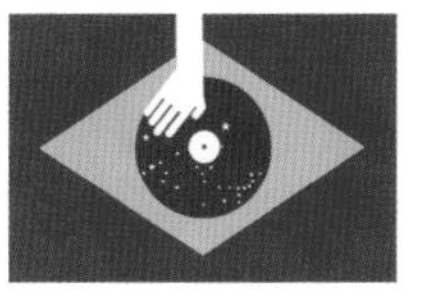	
3 		

1A D Fuego3 C Weapon Records 1B D delit-k-delice C urban records
2A D MEME ENGINE C ANYISM 2B D IMAGWHAUS C University of Minnesota
3A D Carbone Smolan Agency C Chicago Symphony Orchestra 3B D Whaley Design, Ltd C Withrow Ballroom, Katrina Relief Concert

D = Design Firm C = Client

D = Design Firm   C = Client

1A D Savage Synapses Unltd. C Wyclef Jean/Yclef Records 1B D Savage Synapses Unltd. C Wyclef Jean/Yclef Records
2A D Sommese Design C Penn State Jazz Club 2B D Associated Advertising Agency, Inc. C KACY Radio
3A D Associated Advertising Agency, Inc. C KACY Radio 3B D Fox Parlor C Wendy Tremont King

	A	B
1	 	
2		
3		

A

B

1

2

3

1A D Blacktop Creative C American Jazz Museum 1B D Glitschka Studios C Brian Carlson Drumming
2A D Werner Design Werks C VH1 Network 2B D Monster Design Company C Benicia Performing Arts Foundation
3A D Werner Design Werks C Werner Design Werks Inc. 3B D Gardner Design C Russell Public Relations

D = Design Firm C = Client

	A	B
1		
2		
3		

D = Design Firm   C = Client

1A D Henjum Creative C Language Links   1B D Banowetz + Company, Inc. C GLAAD

2A D FUSZION Collaborative C CADCA   2B D Strange Ideas C bad idea

3A D HRM C John E. H. Butler   3B D Steven O'Connor C Cyphon Design

A | B

1

2

3

1A Ⓓ Little Jacket Ⓒ Local Girl Gallery 1B Ⓓ Owen Design Ⓒ Principal
2A Ⓓ Jon Flaming Design Ⓒ Helen Houp 2B Ⓓ Bronson Ma Creative Ⓒ Deep Ellum
3A Ⓓ Davies Associates Ⓒ Cox Paint 3B Ⓓ Crackerbox Ⓒ Gigi Hair Salon

Ⓓ = Design Firm Ⓒ = Client

D = Design Firm C = Client

1A D Tunglid Advertising Agency ehf. C Haircastle 1B D Banowetz + company, Inc. C Dean Banowetz

2A D Gardner Design C A&M Upholstery 2B D ComGroup C Kevin Rowley

3A D Rule29 C Rockport Publishers 3B D Idle Hands Design C student project

	A	B
1		
2		
3		

A

B

1

2

DAVIDSON
ENTERPRISES

ATLAS
BOOKS

3

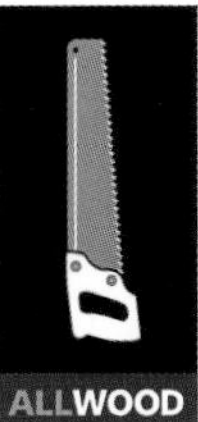

1A Ⓓ Axiom Design Group Ⓒ dataTrust 1B Ⓓ Sergio Bianco Ⓒ romano 1956
2A Ⓓ Brainding Ⓒ Davidson Enterprises 2B Ⓓ Eric Baker Design Assoc. Inc. Ⓒ Atlas Books
3A Ⓓ Wallace Church, Inc. Ⓒ Allwood Construction 3B Ⓓ Zipper Design Ⓒ DINABEAN

Ⓓ = Design Firm Ⓒ = Client

D = Design Firm   C = Client

1A D Brian Sooy & Co. C Black Swamp Percussion 1B D Whaley Design, Ltd C Business Incentives

2A D Blue Tricycle, Inc. C Bursch Brothers, Inc. 2B D Ross Hogin Design C Ray Belisle

3A D Strange Ideas C idea bomb 3B D Strange Ideas C Bad Ideas

	A	B
1		
2		
3	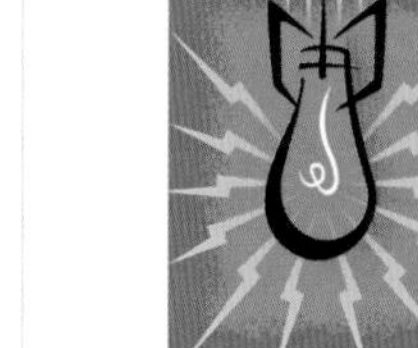	

A

B

1

2

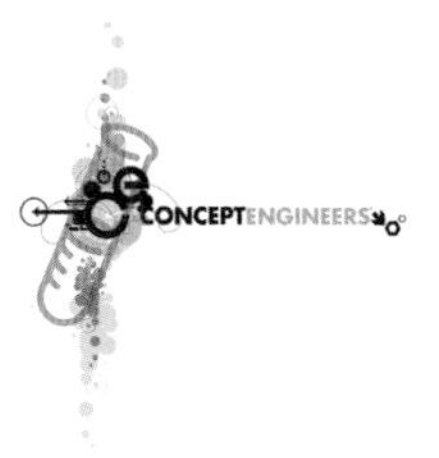

3

1A Ⓓ Dirty Design Ⓒ TC&P 1B Ⓓ Sayles Graphic Design, Inc. Ⓒ Sexicide Band
2A Ⓓ Culture A.D. Ⓒ concept engineers 2B Ⓓ Glitschka Studios Ⓒ Cocoa Labs Software
3A Ⓓ Werner Design Werks Ⓒ Textbooks.com 3B Ⓓ MEME ENGINE Ⓒ ANYISM

Ⓓ = Design Firm Ⓒ = Client

D = Design Firm C = Client

1A D Bull's-Eye Creative Communication C Duo Communications 1B D HuebnerPetersen C Lori Field, Interior Designer
2A D MINE C Brainfloss 2B D Gardner Design C Material Comforts
3A D Glitschka Studios C Christ's Church 3B D Pix Design, inc. C The Woods

	A	B
1		
2	 Brainfloss	
3		 THE WOODS

A B

1

2

3

1A Ⓓ Dotzero Design Ⓒ Boise Paper 1B Ⓓ Les Kerr Creative Ⓒ Wickliffe Land & Cattle Co.
2A Ⓓ Thielen Designs Ⓒ Hyperactive Music Magazine 2B Ⓓ www.iseedots.com Ⓒ Government Executive
3A Ⓓ Archrival Ⓒ Jim Esch for U.S. Congress 3B Ⓓ Strategy Studio Ⓒ Unlock the Block

Ⓓ = Design Firm Ⓒ = Client

Ⓓ = Design Firm Ⓒ = Client

1A Ⓓ Type G Ⓒ Road Runner Sports 1B Ⓓ ellen bruss design Ⓒ Moxie

2A Ⓓ rehab® communication graphics Ⓒ A Little Black Dress 2B Ⓓ Ammunition Ⓒ The Mad Group Ltd

3A Ⓓ Studio Arts and Letters Ⓒ luckybar 3B Ⓓ Deuce Creative Ⓒ Deuce Creative (self-promotion)

A B

1

2

3

	A	B
1		
2		
3		

1A Ⓓ Edward Allen Ⓒ Hyena Editorial 1B Ⓓ Studio Simon Ⓒ Corpus Christi Hooks
2A Ⓓ IMAGEHAUS Ⓒ Far Fetched Spirits 2B Ⓓ Hubbell Design Works Ⓒ Purina Puppy Chow One Year
3A Ⓓ dandy idea Ⓒ DogBoy's Dog Ranch 3B Ⓓ Funk/Levis & Associates, Inc. Ⓒ WetDawg

Ⓓ = Design Firm Ⓒ = Client

Ⓓ = Design Firm Ⓒ = Client

1A Ⓓ Grapefruit Ⓒ Language of the Leaf 1B Ⓓ Strange Ideas Ⓒ Riverside Coffee
2A Ⓓ Strange Ideas Ⓒ coffee icon 2B Ⓓ Strange Ideas Ⓒ cubist coffee
3A Ⓓ Bryan Cooper Design Ⓒ Gold Coast Gourmet Market 3B Ⓓ Visual Inventor Ltd. Co. Ⓒ Fitzgerald Assoc./Brunswick Bowling

	A	B
1	LANGUAGE OF THE LEAF™ *Good tea spoken here*	
2		
3		

A

B

1

2

3

1A Ⓓ Blue Tricycle, Inc. Ⓒ Connect Café, Inc. 1B Ⓓ Barnstorm Creative Group Inc. Ⓒ Wicked Café

2A Ⓓ Strategy Studio Ⓒ Community Café 2B Ⓓ Elephant in the Room Ⓒ Glass Half Full—fundraiser for ALS at local vineyard

3A Ⓓ R&D Thinktank Ⓒ Domaine Haleaux 3B Ⓓ Strange Ideas Ⓒ escape plan

Ⓓ = Design Firm Ⓒ = Client

	A	B
1		
2		
3		

D = Design Firm C = Client

1A D A3 Design C Valley Winery 1B D Rick Johnson & Company C Sigs
2A D Edward Allen C Key Bar 2B D Rick Johnson & Company C OilSlick Imports
3A D Insight Design C My Volunteer Center 3B D Brand Engine C SkylarHaley

A | B

1

2

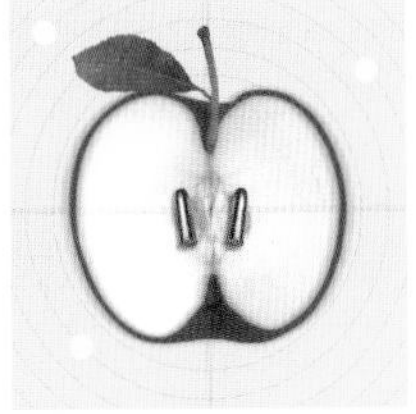

3

all stirred up

1A Ⓓ Werner Design Werks Ⓒ Simple Simon 1B Ⓓ Element Ⓒ Core Financial Services
2A Ⓓ Design Nut Ⓒ Round House Theatre 2B Ⓓ 4sight Communications Ⓒ Moveable Feast
3A Ⓓ MANMADE Ⓒ All Stirred Up 3B Ⓓ David Kampa Ⓒ H.E.B. Foodstores

Ⓓ = Design Firm Ⓒ = Client

Food

A | B

1

LEMON ICE
No 1

2

3

Scallions

D = Design Firm C = Client

1A D Gardner Design C Material Comforts 1B D Delikatessen C Brinkhoffs
2A D Coleman Creative C Hill of Beans Coffee House 2B D Blattner Brunner C Sister's Place, Inc.
3A D UNO C Target Stores 3B D reduced fat C Michele Morris

A B

1

2

3

1A Ⓓ The Envision Group Ⓒ Sweet Peas 1B Ⓓ GingerBee Creative Ⓒ Farm in the Dell
2A Ⓓ Entermotion Design Studio Ⓒ In The Sauce Brands Inc. 2B Ⓓ HMK Archive Ⓒ Anabelle Ardid
3A Ⓓ Special Modern Design Ⓒ Special Modern Design 3B Ⓓ UNO Ⓒ Schreiber Foods

Ⓓ = Design Firm Ⓒ = Client

Ⓓ = Design Firm Ⓒ = Client

1A Ⓓ silvercreativegroup Ⓒ Tim Smith 1B Ⓓ Steve's Portfolio Ⓒ Sweet Dreams Bakery
2A Ⓓ David Kampa Ⓒ H.E.B. Foodstores 2B Ⓓ Hallmark Cards Inc. Ⓒ A La Mode
3A Ⓓ Hayes + Company Ⓒ Liberty Village BIA 3B Ⓓ Actual Size Creative Ⓒ Roadside Ribs

	A	B
1	CHEESESMITH	sweet dreams bakery
2		
3	Here Comes SUMMER	

A B

1

2

3

·LAVITA É BELLA·

1A Ⓓ Bryan Cooper Design Ⓒ Wiener Works 1B Ⓓ GSD&M Ⓒ Texas BBQ Academy
2A Ⓓ Landor Associates Ⓒ Baked Lays 2B Ⓓ Tribe Design Houston Ⓒ Dart Pizza
3A Ⓓ Nick Glenn Design Ⓒ Zeek's Pizzeria 3B Ⓓ urbanINFLUENCE design studio Ⓒ LaVita é Bella Ristorante

Ⓓ = Design Firm Ⓒ = Client

Ⓓ = Design Firm Ⓒ = Client

1A Ⓓ ellen bruss design Ⓒ The Oven Pizza e Vino 1B Ⓓ M3 Advertising Design Ⓒ toss restaurant
2A Ⓓ Farah Design, Inc. Ⓒ San Antonio Wine 2B Ⓓ Actual Size Creative Ⓒ Soirée Catering
3A Ⓓ 4sight Communications Ⓒ Moveable Feast 3B Ⓓ Fauxkoi Ⓒ Lara Miklasevics

	A	B
1	the oven PIZZA E VINO	
2		
3		

A | B |
--- | --- | ---

1

women on the edge
washington professionals
dishing over lunch

2

3

1A Ⓓ Wallace Church, Inc. Ⓒ TizNow Restaurant 1B Ⓓ BatesNeimand Ⓒ BatesNeimand
2A Ⓓ Diagram Ⓒ Culinaria Restaurant 2B Ⓓ GSD&M Ⓒ Jackpot Buffet
3A Ⓓ idGO Advertising Ⓒ Meal Works 3B Ⓓ Sandstrom Design Ⓒ Noodlin'

Ⓓ = Design Firm Ⓒ = Client

A B

1

2

3

D = Design Firm C = Client

1A D Timpano Group C Healthy Home Reports 1B D Entermotion Design Studio C Digital Brand
2A D Boelts/Stratford Associates C Renter Rights 2B D Mirko Ilić Corp C The Orphan Society of America
3A D Yellow Fin Studio C Housing Works—Austin 3B D A3 Design C Mattamy Homes

	A	B
1		
2		
3		

1A D Savage Design Group C The Joy School 1B D Paul Black Design C Centex
2A D Blattner Brunner C Beacon House 2B D Jason Pillon C Dawn Marie-Tragoutsis
3A D Fernandez Design C eTrust 3B D Carol Gravelle Graphic Design C Fidelity National Real Estate Solutions

D = Design Firm C = Client

ⓓ = Design Firm ⓒ = Client

1A ⓓ Sire advertising ⓒ Harie Insurance Exchange 1B ⓓ Actual Size creative ⓒ unused

2A ⓓ Dotzero Design ⓒ Office of Sustainable Dev. 2B ⓓ Design One ⓒ Isgrid Mortgage Group

3A ⓓ Brook Group, LTD ⓒ House of Ruth, Maryland 3B ⓓ marc usa ⓒ Indianapolis Neighborhood Housing Partners

	A	B
1		
2		
3	  	

A | B

1

2

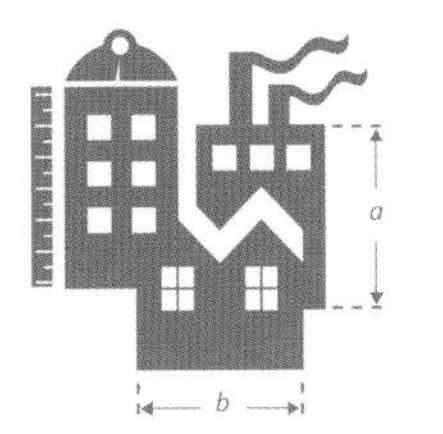

3

1A Ⓓ Ross Hogin Design Ⓒ Domicile Properties 1B Ⓓ Dotzero Design Ⓒ Office of Sustainable Dev.
2A Ⓓ Yellobee Studio Ⓒ Via Elisa 2B Ⓓ Gridwerk Ⓒ ReaStat, Inc.
3A Ⓓ Design Nut Ⓒ Council for Advancement & Support of Education 3B Ⓓ C.Cady Design Ⓒ Autodesk

Ⓓ = Design Firm Ⓒ = Client

Ⓓ = Design Firm Ⓒ = Client

1A Ⓓ jsDesignCo. Ⓒ Throttle, LTD. 1B Ⓓ Special Modern Design Ⓒ Los Angeles Conservancy's Modern Committee
2A Ⓓ Harkey Design Ⓒ Handyman Atlanta 2B Ⓓ 1 Trick Pony Ⓒ Gotham Sound & Communications, Inc.
3A Ⓓ Edward Allen Ⓒ GSD&M 3B Ⓓ Banowetz + Company, Inc. Ⓒ Monica Greene / Cuidad

	A	B
1		
2		
3		

	A	B
1		
2		
3		

1A D Emphasize LLC C Police Department San Andrés Island 1B D Cfx C Jones Lang Lasalle
2A D Hinge C Clark Realty 2B D JC Thomas Marketing/Advertising C Potter Construction
3A D Schuster Design Group C Docupresence 3B D Bright Strategic Design C Lee Homes

D = Design Firm C = Client

Ⓓ = Design Firm   Ⓒ = Client

1A Ⓓ Cfx Ⓒ Howard Commercial Realty 1B Ⓓ UlrichPinciotti Design Group Ⓒ self
2A Ⓓ emblem Ⓒ Alcaldia de Chacao 2B Ⓓ Gardner Design Ⓒ Russell Public Relations
3A Ⓓ Design Nut Ⓒ Colonial Beach Baptist Church 3B Ⓓ Blue Tricycle, Inc. Ⓒ Escapes to New York

	A	B
1		
2		
3		

A

B

1

2

3

1A Ⓓ Gee + Chung Design Ⓒ 3D Motion 1B Ⓓ Jonathan Rice & Company Ⓒ Highrises.com
2A Ⓓ Erick Baker Design Assoc. Inc. Ⓒ Gotham Books 2B Ⓓ STUN Design and Advertising Ⓒ LA Politics
3A Ⓓ Think Tank Creative Ⓒ Our Savior's Church 3B Ⓓ Sabingrafik, Inc. Ⓒ Portola Springs

Ⓓ = Design Firm Ⓒ = Client

Structures

A | B

Ⓓ = Design Firm Ⓒ = Client

1A Ⓓ Sergio Bianco Ⓒ Amici degli Uffizi 1B Ⓓ LogDesignSource.com Ⓒ Bonjour de Paris
2A Ⓓ judson design associates Ⓒ unused 2B Ⓓ Jon Flaming Design Ⓒ Proposed Castle Mailing Services
3A Ⓓ Uhlein Design Ⓒ Passic County New Jersey Film Commission 3B Ⓓ Hanna & Associates Ⓒ Castle Rock Masonry

1

UFFIZI
GALLERY

2

K
KIRBYLOFTS

3

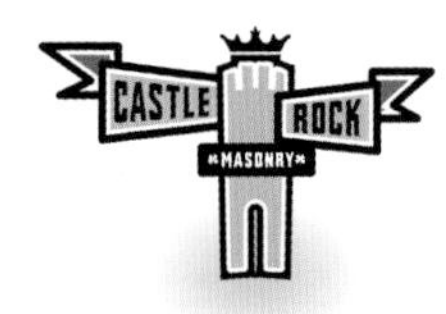

A

B

1

2

3

1A D Edward Allen C Everythinghome 1B D Sockeye Creative C Game Crazy
2A D The Oesterle C Affilinet 2B D Sakkal Design C Lusaka Muslim Association
3A D GSD&M C Alamo Hotels 3B D Hubbell Design Works C Fireball Bowling

D = Design Firm C = Client

D = Design Firm   C = Client

1A D Werner Design Werks C Archer Farms for Target Stores 1B D Gee + Chung Design C Sun Microsystems
2A D Maycreate C Whitehall Properties 2B D Whitney Edwards LLC C Eastern Shore Title Company
3A D GSD&M C City of Austin 3B D Bemporad Baranowski Marketing Group C Robert Wood Johnson Health Policy Fellowships Program

	A	B
1	Archer Farms	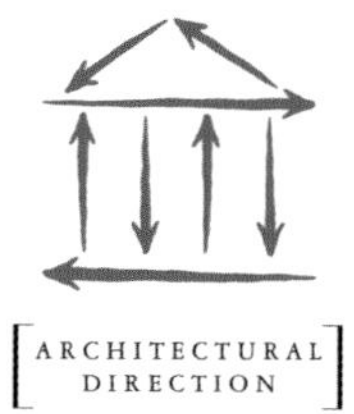
2		 Eastern Shore Title Company
3		 HEALTH POLICY FELLOWSHIPS PROGRAM

A B

1

TANDEM
marketing

2

3

1A Ⓓ Corduroy Ⓒ Tandem Marketing 1B Ⓓ maximo, inc. Ⓒ Frontera de Ceramica
2A Ⓓ Werner Design Werks Ⓒ Textbooks.com 2B Ⓓ Owen Design Ⓒ Inner Flora
3A Ⓓ David Russell Design Ⓒ Mucci Trucksess Architecture and Interiors 3B Ⓓ Ramp Ⓒ Mark Steward Securities

Ⓓ = Design Firm Ⓒ = Client

	A	B
1		
2		
3		

D = Design Firm C = Client

1A D www.iseedots.com C Vertex Studios 1B D nicelogo.com C Clegg
2A D Strategy Studio C Tucker Anthony Sutro 2B D Axiom Design Group C Yokahama University
3A D Dashwood Design Ltd C Rubicon 3B D CAPSULE C CapsuleShak

A | B

1

2

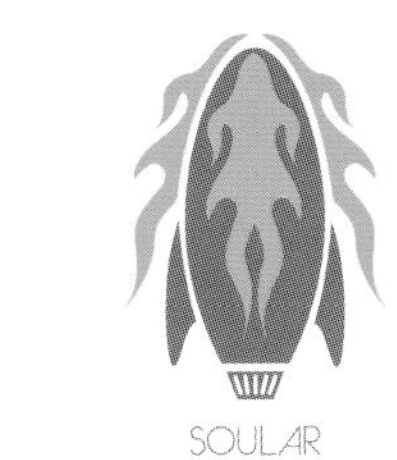

3

1A Ⓓ Strange Ideas Ⓒ rocket coffee 1B Ⓓ Mez Design Ⓒ Rocket Opera
2A Ⓓ Thielen Designs Ⓒ Soular 2B Ⓓ Zwölf Sonnen Ⓒ Red Rocket
3A Ⓓ Brand navigation Ⓒ Transit 3B Ⓓ davpunk! Ⓒ Propulsion Media

Ⓓ = Design Firm Ⓒ = Client

Transportation

A | B

1

Ocotillo
TEST RANGE

2

ascentives
corporate speciality solutions

3

D = Design Firm   C = Client

1A D MINE C Omega High Power Rocketry 1B D Mires C Ocotillo
2A D HardBall Sports C Bestnotes 2B D Rule29 C Ascentives
3A D Alesce C The Creative Alliance 3B D The Meyocks Group C West Metro Airport

A | B

1

2

3

1A Ⓓ Strange Ideas Ⓒ Wichita Aviation Festival 1B Ⓓ VMA Ⓒ Huffy Bicycle Company
2A Ⓓ Tim Frame Design Ⓒ Touristees.com 2B Ⓓ Mires Ⓒ Eric Lobello
3A Ⓓ The Logo Factory Inc. Ⓒ Bridgehampton Motoring Club 3B Ⓓ Edward Allen Ⓒ Speed Bar

Ⓓ = Design Firm Ⓒ = Client

A | B

Ⓓ = Design Firm   Ⓒ = Client

1A Ⓓ Edward Allen Ⓒ House O' Speed   1B Ⓓ Jon Flaming Design Ⓒ Red Cab Design
2A Ⓓ Fresh Oil Ⓒ AudioStop   2B Ⓓ Felixsockwell.com Ⓒ Goodwill Industries
3A Ⓓ Sterling Brands Ⓒ Artwagen   3B Ⓓ judson design associates Ⓒ The Glasswall Restaurant

1

2

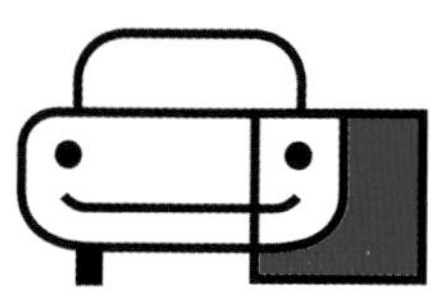

3

A B

1

2

3

1A D sheean design C Unfiltered Napa 1B D Ross Creative + Strategy C We Care Transport
2A D Sockeye Creative C Red Truck Publishing 2B D GSD&M C Trout Trucking
3A D TBF Creative C Bak-A-Bush Adventures 3B D Reynolds + Associates C Indianapolis Police Motorcycle Drill Team

D = Design Firm C = Client

Ⓓ = Design Firm Ⓒ = Client

1A Ⓓ Matt Whitley Ⓒ Indy Motor Speedway 1B Ⓓ Brainding Ⓒ Motorcycle

2A Ⓓ R&R Partners Ⓒ Moto Logo 2B Ⓓ R&R Partners Ⓒ Throttle 2

3A Ⓓ Motorcycle Safety Foundation Ⓒ Scooter School 3B Ⓓ David Kampa Ⓒ Texas Bicycle Coalition

	A	B
1	INDIANAPOLIS 500	MotoRecycle
2		
3		

A | B

1 

2

L'Arcavolo

3

1A Ⓓ Greg Walters Design Ⓒ BreakAway Consulting 1B Ⓓ Sandstrom Design Ⓒ adidas
2A Ⓓ Strange Ideas Ⓒ shark racing 2B Ⓓ Howling Good Designs Ⓒ Spokeswomen Cycling Team
3A Ⓓ Studio GT&P Ⓒ Tessuti di Montefalco Srl 3B Ⓓ octane inc. Ⓒ Carolina Heritage Line

Ⓓ = Design Firm Ⓒ = Client

D = Design Firm C = Client

1A D Miles Design C Java Train 1B D Praxis Studios C Five Star Restaurant
2A D Formikula C Die Artillerie 2B D Stiles Design C Sounds From Home
3A D octane inc. C JB Communications 3B D FUSZION Collaborative C Atlantis Events

	A	B
1		FIVE STAR
2		
3	 	

A | B |
--- | --- | ---
 |  | 1
 |  | 2
 |  | 3

1A Ⓓ Eisenberg and Associates Ⓒ Seven Ships 1B Ⓓ Sandstrom Design Ⓒ Full Sail

2A Ⓓ Bryan Cooper Design Ⓒ The Center for the Physically Challenged 2B Ⓓ Nick Glenn Design Ⓒ Seven Seafood Bar and Grill

3A Ⓓ Gardner Design Ⓒ Navential 3B Ⓓ Gee + Chung Design Ⓒ Castile Ventures

Ⓓ = Design Firm Ⓒ = Client

Ⓓ = Design Firm Ⓒ = Client

1A Ⓓ Ramp Ⓒ Viking Star Enterprises 1B Ⓓ Stephan and Herr Ⓒ AMP Incorporated
2A Ⓓ Fresh Oil Ⓒ 22 Bowen's Wine Bar & Grille 2B Ⓓ Sabingrafik, Inc. Ⓒ Sempra Energy
3A Ⓓ Harkey Design Ⓒ Snug Harbour 3B Ⓓ northfound Ⓒ Catering St. Louis

	A	B
1		
2		
3		

index

directory

(twentystar)
United States
303.596.4134
www.twentystar.com

1 Trick Pony
United States
646.485.8831
www.1trickpony.com

28 LIMITED BRAND
Germany
49.20.939.4238
www.mircommedia.de

2cdesign
United States
214.599.9078
www.2cdesign

343 Creative
United States
718.720.7779
www.343creative.com

38one
United Kingdom
44.79.6823.8671
www.38one.com

4sight Communication
United States
323.954.3550
www.get4sight.com

68Design
United States
404.861.5756
www.68design.com

9fps
United States
312.697.1530
www.9fps.net

9MYLES, Inc.
United States
858.344.8619
www.9myles.com

A3 Design
United States
704.568.5351
www.athreedesign.com

Abiah
United States
609.653.2233
www.abiah.com

Actual Size Creative
United States
412.421.3279
www.thisisactualsize.com

adbass:designs LLC
United States
516.285.0385
www.adbassdesigns.com

Addison Whitney
United States
704.347.5700
www.addisonwhitney.com

AKOFA Creative
United States
404.915.8127
www.akofa.com

Alesce
United States
303.229.8100
www.alesce.com

Ali Cindoruk
United States
212.673.5517
www.alicindoruk.com

Allen Creative
United States
770.972.8862
www.allencreative.com

Alphabet Arm Design
United States
617.451.9990
www.alphabetarmdesign.com

America Online
United States
614.538.4632
www.netscape.com

Ammunition
United Kingdom
44.207.241.2233
www.ammunition.uk

amyHELLER design
United States
203.773.1988
www.amyhellerdesign.com

angryporcupine*design
United States
435.655.0645
www.angryporcupine.com

Anoroc
United States
919.821.1191
www.anorocagency.com

Archrival
United States
402.435.2525
www.archrival.com

Ardoise Design
Canada
514.287.1002
www.ardoise.com

Armeilia Subianto Design
Indonesia
62.21.527.4364
www.asubiantodesign.com

ArtGraphics.ru
Russia
7.095.730.5233
www.artgraphics.ru

ASGARD
Russia
7.812.389.0631
www.asgard-design.com

Associated Advertising Agency, Inc.
United States
316.683.4691
www.associatedadv.com

Atha Design
United States
641.673.2820

Aurora Design
United States
518.346.6228
www.auroradesignonline.com

Axiom Design Group
United States
713.523.5711
www.axiomdg.com

Axiom Design Partners
Western Australia
618.9381.6270
www.axiomdp.com.au

B.L.A. Design Company
United States
803.518.4130

b5 Marketing & Kommunikation GmbH
Germany
49.06201.8790731
www.b5-media.de

baba designs
United States
248.360.1251
www.anniewidmyer.com

Bakken Creative Co.
United States
510.540.8260
www.bakkencreativeco.com

Banowetz + Company, Inc.
United States
214.823.7300
www.banowetz.com

Barnstorm Creative
United States
719.630.7200
www.barnstormcreative.biz

Barnstorm Creative Group Inc.
Canada
604.681.3377
www.barnstormcreative.com

batesneimand inc.
United States
202.637.9732
www.batesneimand.com

BCM/D
United States
410.290.5290

Bemporad Baranowski Marketing Group
United States
212.473.4902
www.bbmg.com

Big Bald Guy Design Studio
United States
303.843.9777
www.envision-grp.com

Blacktop Creative
United States
816.221.1585
www.blacktopcreative.com

Blattner Brunner
United States
412.995.9585
www.blattnerbrunner.com

BLOOM LLC
United States
415.451.1866
www.bloommedia.com

Blue Storm Design
New Zealand
644.562.8771
www.bluestormdesign.co.nz

Blue Studios, Inc.
United States
410.342.3600
www.bluestudios.com

Blue Tricycle, Inc.
United States
612.729.2372
www.bluetricycle.com

Boelts/Stratford Associates
United States
520.792.1026
www.boeltsstratford.com

Bonilla Design
United States
847.791.3491

Boom Creative
United States
216.291.2411
www.boom-creative.com

Born to Design
United States
317.838.9404
www.born-to-design.com

Brady Design Ltd
United States
614.299.6661
www.bradydesignltd.com

Brainding
United States
305.921.9583
www.brainding.com.ar

Brand Bird
United States
404.373.2950
www.brandbird.com

Brand Engine
United States
415.339.4220
www.brandengine.com

Brand Navigation
United States
541.549.4425
www.brandnavigation.com

Brandesign
United States
609.490.9700
www.brandesign.com

Brandia
Portugal
351.213.923000
www.brandia.net

Brandient
Romania
40.21.222.8167
www.brandient.com

BrandSavvy, Inc.
United States
303.471.9991
www.brandsavvyinc.com

Braue; Branding & Corporate Design
Germany
49.471.983820
www.braue.info

Brian Blankenship
United States
817.917.8379
www.brianblankenship.com

Brian Collins Design
United States
417.890.5933
www.williamscollins.com

Brian Sooy & Co.
United States
440.322.5142
www.briansooy.com

Bright Strategic Design
United States
310.305.2565
www.brightdesign.com

Bristol-Myers Squibb Company
United States
609.897.3143
www.bms.com

Bronson Ma Creative
United States
214.457.5615
www.bronsonma.com

Brook Group, LTD
United States
410.465.7805
www.brookgroup.com

Bryan Cooper Design
United States
918.732.3333
www.bryancooperdesign.com
www.cooperillustration.com

Bull's-Eye Creative Communications
United States
404.352.3006
www.bullseyecreativecommunications
.com

Bunch
Croatia
385.14.920855
www.bunchdesign.com

C. Cady Design
United States
423.843.0456
www.ccadydesign.com

Campbell Fisher Design
United States
602.955.2707
www.thinkcfd.com

CAPSULE
United States
612.341.4525
www.capsule.us

Carbone Smolan Agency
United States
212.807.0011
www.carbonsmolan.com

Carol Gravelle Graphic Design
United States
805.383.2773
www.carolgravelledesign.com

Catch Design Studio
United States
206.322.4323
www.catchstudio.com

Cato Purnell Partners
Australia
61.3.9429.6577
www.catopartners.com

cc design
United States
423.926.3737

CDI Studios
United States
702.876.3316
www.cdistudios.com

Cfx
United States
314.968.1161
www.cfx-inc.com

CH & LER Design
United States
801.966.9171

Chad Carr Design/Westcarr
United States
612.331.4350
www.westcarr.com

Cheri Gearhart, graphic design
United States
708.34634855
www.gearhartdesign.com

Chimera Design
Australia
61.3.9593.6844
www.chimera.com.au

Chris Malven Design
United States
515.450.9023
www.chrismalven.com

christiansen: creative
United States
715.381.8480
www.christiansencreative.com

Church Logo Gallery
United States
760.231.9368
www.churchlogogallery.com

Cisneros Design
United States
505.471.6699
www.cisnerosdesign.com

Clark Studios
United States
949.351.5925
www.clark-studios.com

Coleman Creative
United States
832.797.1682

Colle + McVoy
United States
952.852.7500
www.collemcvoy.com

ComGroup
United States
404.892.4474
www.comgroupmra.com

Communique Group
United States
303.220.5080
www.thecommuniquegroup.com

CONCEPTiCONS
United States
818.259.2725
www.concepticons.com

concussion, llc
United States
817.336.6824
www.concussion.net

Corduroy
United States
214.827.3007
www.corduroydesign.com

Corporate Express
United States
303.664.2000
www.CorporateExpress.com

Cotterteam
United States
410.276.3794
www.nitrobranddesign.com

Crackerbox
United States
617.437.7549
www.crackerbox.us

Creative Kong
United States
512.589.6160
www.creativekong.com

CS Design
United States
320.493.5854

Culture A.D.
United States
404.230.9339
www.culture-ad.com

Curtis Sayers Design
United States
617.947.2720
www.csayersdesign.com

Curtis Sharp Design
United States
206.366.7975
www.curtissharpdesign.com

d4 creative group
United States
215.483.4555
www.d4creative.com

dale harris
Australia
041.189.9840
www.daleharris.com

Dan Rood Design
United States
785.842.4870
www.danrooddesign.com

dandy idea
United States
512.627.9103
www.dandyidea.com

Dashwood Design Ltd
New Zealand
0064.9307.0901
www.dashwooddesign.com.nz

David Kampa
United States
512.636.3791
www.kampadesign.com

David Maloney Design
United States
612.396.2548
www.david-maloney.com

David Russell Design
United States
206.621.1360
www.davidrusselldesign.com

Davies Associates
United States
310.247.9572
www.daviesla.com

davpunk!
United States
847.345.7865
www.davpunk.com

Day Six Creative
United States
972.548.7337
www.daysixcreative.com

DDB
United States
312.552.6124
www.ddb.com

DDB Dallas
United States
214.259.4200
www.ddbdallas.com

dedstudios
United States
310.850.2161

Deep Design
United States
404.266.7500
www.deepdesign.com

Delikatessen
Germany
0049.40.350.8060
www.delikatessen-hamburg.com

delit-k-delice
France
33.1.499.771.984
www.absolutely-design.com

Design and Image
United States
303.292.3455
www.designandimage.com

Design MG/DMG
Panama
507.214.1781.1700

Design Nut
United States
301.942.2360
www.designnut.com

Design One
United States
828.254.7898
www.d1inc.com

designlab, inc
United States
314.962.7702
www.designlabinc.com

Designsensory
United States
865.690.2249
www.designsensory.com

design-studio Muhina
Russia
7.3412.76.3315
www.muhina.com

Deuce Creative
United States
713.863.8633
www.deucecreative.com

Device
United Kingdom
347.535.0626

Diagram
Poland
48.61.664.8081
www.diagram.pl

Dialekt Design
Canada
450.226.1440
www.dialektdesign.com

DIRECT DESIGN Visual Branding
Russia
7.095.916.01.23
www.directdesign.ru

Dirty Design
United Kingdom
44.0.117.927.3344
www.dirtydesign.co.uk

Ditto!
United States
914.478.3641
www.dittodoesit.com

dmayne design
United States
417.823.8058
www.dmaynedesign.com

Doink, Inc.
United States
305.529.0121
www.doinkdesign.com

Dotfive
United States
415.354.1076
www.dotfive.com

Dotzero Design
United States
503.892.9262
www.DotzeroDesign.com

Doug Beatty
Canada
416.826.3684
www.taxizone.com

Dr. Alderete
Mexico
5255.1998.4688
www.jorgealderete.com

Dreamedia Studios
United States
501.954.9711
www.dreamediastudios.com

Duffy & Partners
United States
612.548.2333
www.duffy.com

Eben Design
United States
206.523.9010
www.ebendesign.com

Edward Allen
United States
512.443.2102

eindruck design
United States
406.829.1581
www.eindruckdesign.com

Eisenberg and Associates
United States
214.528.5990
www.eisenberg-inc.com

Elaine Park
United States
312.384.1906
www.commongroundmktg.com

element
United States
614.447.0906
www.elementville.com

Elephant in the Room
United States
336.624.9844
www.elephantintheroom.biz

Eleven Feet Media
United States
650.278.2451
www.elevenfeetmedia.com

elf design
United States
650.358.9973
www.elf-design.com

ellen bruss design
United States
303.830.8323
www.ebd.com

emblem
Venezuela
58.212.243.2969
www.mblm.com

Emphasize LLC
United States
718.932.7810
www.mariavilla.com

Entermotion Design Studio
United States
316.264.2277
www.entermotion.com

Enterprise
South Africa
27.11.319.8000
www.enterpriseig.co.zg

Eric Baker Design Assoc. Inc.
United States
212.598.9111
www.ericbakerdesign.com

Exti Dzyn
United States
818.679.9116
www.extidzyn.com

Eyebeam Creative LLC
United States
202.518.5888
www.eyebeamcreative.com

Eyescape
United Kingdom
44.0.20.8521.0342
www.eyescape.co.uk

fallindesign studio
Russia
7.812.461.1985
www.faldin.ru

Farah Design, Inc.
United States
786.267.2954
www.farahdesign.com &
www.visiom.com

Farm Design
United States
310.828.1624
www.farmdesign.net

Fauxkoi
United States
612.251.4277
www.fauxkoi.com

Felixsockwell.com
United States
917.657.8880
www.felixsockwell.com

Fernandez Design
United States
512.619.4020
www.fernandezdesign.com

Fifth Letter
United States
336.723.5655
www.fifth-letter.com

FigDesign
United States
972.259.5900
www.figdesign.com

FiveStone
United States
678.730.0686
www.FiveStone.com

Flaxenfield, Inc.
United States
336.218.0530
www.flaxenfield.com

Floor 84 Studio
United States
818.754.1231
www.floor84studio.com

Formikula
Germany
49.0.89.48.00.45.64
www.marc-herold.com

Fox Parlor
United States
415.821.7100
www.foxparlor.com

Franke+Fiorella
United States
612.338.1700
www.frankefiorella.com

Fredrik Lewander
Sweden
46.73.955.9968
www.fredriklewander.se

Fresh Oil
United States
401.709.4656
www.freshoil.com

Freshwater Design
United States
678.910.6381
www.freshwaterdesign.net

Fuego3
United States
817.937.1605
www.fuego3.com

Funk/Levis & Associates, Inc
United States
541.485.1932
www.funklevis.com

FUSZION Collaborative
United States
703.548.8080
www.fuszion.com

FutureBrand
United States
212.931.6300
www.futurebrand.com

FutureBrand Melbourne
Australia
613.9604.2777
www.futurebrand.com

FutureBrand Buenos Aires
5411.4777.2277
www.futurebrand.com

Fuze
United States
775.626.4577
www.ifuze.com

FWIS
United States
503.230.1741
www.fwis.com

Gabi Toth
Romania
4.072.253.3715
www.toth.ro

Gabriel Kalach*V I S U A L communications
United States
305.532.2336

Gabriela Gasparini Design
United States
718.417.1064
www.gabrielagasparini.com

Gardner Design
United States
316.691.8808
www.gardnerdesign.com

Garfinkel Design
United States
706.369.6831
www.garfinkeldesign.com

Gee + Chung Design
United States
415.543.1192
www.geechungdesign.com

Gee Creative
United States
843.853.3086
www.geecreative.com

GetElevatedDesign.com
United States
www.ejhartley.com

ginger griffin marketing and design
United States
704.896.2479
www.wehaveideas.com

GingerBee Creative
United States
406.443.3032
www.gingerbee.com

Glitschka Studios
United States
971.223.6143
www.vonglitschka.com

Goldforest
United States
305.573.7370
www.goldforest.com

GRAF d'SIGN creative boutique
Russia
7.916.686.2812
www.gdscb.com

GrafiQa Graphic Design
United States
607.433.8837
www.grafiqa.com

Grapefruit
Romania
40.232.233.066

Greg Walters Design
United States
206.362.1310

greteman group
United States
316.263.1004
www.gretemangroup.com

Gridwerk
United States
215.872.6266
www.gridwerk.net

GSCS
United Arab Emirates
971.4391.0873
www.greggsedgwick.com

GSD&M
United States
512.242.4602
www.gsdm.com

Hallmark Cards Inc.
United States
816.545.6753
www.hallmark.com

Hammerpress
United States
816.421.1929
www.hammerpress.net

Hanna & Associates
United States
208.661.9455
www.cdaoriginals.com

HardBall Sports
United States
904.998.8778
www.hardballcreative.com

Harkey Design
United States
404.609.9090
www.harkeydesign.com

Harwood Kirsten Leigh McCoy
South Africa
27.83.441.0174
www.hklm.co.za

Hausch Design Agency LLC
United States
414.628.3976
www.hauschdesign.com

Hayes + Company
Canada
416.536.5438
www.hayesandcompany.com

Henjum Creative
United States
920.866.3738

Hill Design Studios
United States
503.507.1228
www.hilldesignstudios.com

Hinge
United States
703.391.8870
www.pivotalbrands.com

Hipflix.com/The 5659 Design Co.
United States
773.685.7019
www.hipflix.com

Hirshorn Zuckerman Design Group
United States
301.294.6302

HMK Archive
United States
210.473.1961
www.sharkthang.com

Honey Design
Canada
519.679.0786
www.honey.on.ca

Hope Advertising
Australia
613.9529.7799
www.hope.com.au

Hornall Anderson
United States
206.826.2329
www.hadw.com

Howerton + White Interactive
United States
316.262.6644
www.howertonwhite.com

Howling Good Designs
United States
631.427.4769
www.howlinggooddesigns.com

Hoyne Design
Australia
61.39.537.1822
www.hoyne.com.au

HRM
United States
985.879.2443
www.hrmcreative.com

Hubbell Design Works
United States
714.227.3457
www.hubbelldesignworks.com

HuebnerPetersen
United States
970.663.9344

humanot
716.604.4026
www.humanot.com

Hutchinson Associates, Inc.
United States
312.455.9191
www.hutchinson.com

i3design
United States
610.828.6442
www.i3design.us

i4 Solutions
United States
801.294.6400
www.i4.net

Idea Girl Design
United States
310.623.2288
www.ideagirldesign.com

idGO Advertising
United States
401.368.1049

Idle Hands Design
United States
917.690.2383
www.idlehandsnyc.com

Ikola designs
United States
763.533.3440

IMA Design, Corp.
Russia
7.095.262.5985
www.Imadesign.ru

IMAGEHAUS
United States
612.377.8700
www.imagehaus.net

Imaginaria
United States
214.257.8704
www.imaginariacreative.com

INNFUSION Studios
United States
800.996.7616
www.innfusionstudios.com

Insight Design
United States
316.262.0085

Insomniac Creative Studio
United States
www.insomniaccs.com

Integer Group - Midwest
United States
515.288.7910
www.interger.com

Interrobang Design Collaborative, Inc.
United States
802.434.5970
www.interrobangdesign.com

Intersection Creative
United States
602.622.8757
www.intersectioncreative.com

Iperdesign, Inc.
United States
917.412.9045
www.iperdesign.com

ivan2design
United States
206.364.8996
www.ivan2.com

j6Studios
www.j6studios.com

Jason Kirshenblatt/The O Group
United States
212.398.0100

www.ogroup.net
Jason Pillon
United States
925.243.1936

JC Thomas Marketing/Advertising
United States
704.377.9660
www.thoughtville.com

Jeff Pollard Design
United States
503.246.7251
www.jpd-logos.com

Jejak, Rumah Iklan dan Disain
Indonesia
62.21.722.3306
www.jejak.net

Jenny Kolcun Freelance Design
United States
415.331.7202

joe miller's company
United States
408.988.2924

Joi Design
New Zealand
649.377.6684
www.joi.co.nz

Jon Flaming Design
United States
972.235.4880
www.jonflaming.com

Jonathan Rice & Company
United States
817.886.6640
www.jriceco.com

josh higgins design
United States
619.379.2090
www.joshhiggins.com

joven orozco design
United States
949.723.1898
www.jovenville.com

jsDesignCo.
United States
614.353.6412

judson design associates
United States
713.520.1096
www.judsondesign.com

juls design inc
United States
515.963.8309
www.julsdesign.com

Justin Johnson
United States
918.519.1605
www.morebranding.com

Justin Lockwood Design
United States
206.529.7585
www.justinlockwooddesign.com

Kahn Design
United States
760.944.5574
www.kahn-design.com

Kaimere
United Arab Emirates
971.4391.8083
www.tmh.ae

Kendall Creative Shop, Inc.
United States
214.827.6680
www.kendallcreative.com

Kendall Ross
United States
206.262.0540
www.kendallross.com

Kern Design Group
United States
203.329.7070
www.kerndesigngroup.com

Kevin France Design, Inc.
United States
336.765.6213

Keyword Design
United States
219.923.5279
www.keyworddesign.com

Kinesis, Inc.
United States
541.482.3600
www.kinesisinc.com

Kineto
Indonesia
62.21.831.7106
www.kineto.biz

Kitemath
United States
773.252.9908
www.kitemath.com

KOESTER design
United States
469.621.6566
www.koesterdesign.com

KONG Design Group
United States
714.478.9657
www.kongdesigngroup.com

KURT FOR HIRE
United States
917.771.4142
www.kurtforhire.com

KW43 BRANDDESIGN
Germany
49.200.557.7830
www.kw43.gr

Kym Abrams Design
United States
312.654.1005
www.kad.com

label brand
United States
831.421.0518
www.labelbrand.com

Lance Reed/tmh the Media House
United Arab Emirates
971.4391.8083
www.tmh.ae

LandDesign
United States
703.549.7784
www.landdesign.com

Landkamer Partners, Inc.
United States
415.522.2480
www.landkamerpartners.com

Landor Associates
United States
212.614.5261
www.landor.com

Lars Lawson
United States
317.921.0948
www.timberdesignco.com

Lauchpad Creative
United States
405.514.5158
www.launchpad321.com

Leeann Leftwich Zajas Graphic Design
United States
603.702.1044
www.11zdesign.com

Lenox Graphics
United States
401.862.7224
www.lenoxgraphics.com

Les Kerr Creative
United States
972.236.3599
www.leskerr.net

Lesniewicz Associates
United States
419.243.7131
www.designtoinfluence.com

Letter 7
United States
212.595.7445
www.ltr7.com

Lienhart Design
United States
312.738.2200
www.lienhartdesign.com

Lippincott Mercer
United States
212.521.0000
www.lippincottmercer.com

Lisa Speer
United States
917.533.6397
www.lisaspeer.com

Lisa Starace
United States
619.757.6308
www.designactionism.com

Liska + Associates Communication Design
United States
312.644.4400
www.liska.com

Little Jacket
United States
216.373.6979
www.little-jacket.com

Living Creative Design
United States
510.304.0450
www.LivingCreative.com

Lizette Gecel
United States
804.359.1711

logobyte design studio
Turkey
90.535.666.6292
www.logobyte.com

LogoDesignSource.com
United States
954.428.8871
www.logodesignsource.com

Lulu Strategy
United States
614.221.3403
www.lulustrategy.com

Lunar Cow
United States
800.594.9620
www.lunarcow.com

Lunar Design
United States
415.252.4388
www.lunar.com

M3 Advertising Design
United States
702.796.6323
www.m3ad.com

Macnab Design Visual Communication
United States
508.286.8558
www.macnabdesign.com

Mad Dog Graphx
United States
907.276.5062
www.thedogpack.com

MANMADE
United States
415.865.9996
www.manmade.com

MannPower Design
United States
973.983.0626
www.mannpowerdesign.com

marc usa
United States
317.632.6501
www.marcusa.com

Maremar Graphic Design
Puerto Rico
787.731.8795
www.maremar.com

Mariqua Design
United States
650.242.4645
www.mariqua.com

markatos
United States
415.235.9203
www.markatos.com

Mary Hutchison Design LLC
United States
206.407.3460
www.maryhutchisondesign.com

Matt Everson Design
United States
608.628.3095
www.matteverson.com

Matt Whitley/Outdoor Cap
United States
479.464.5203
www.outdoorcap.com

mattisimo
United States
415.786.2769
www.mattisimo.com

Mattson Creative
United States
949.388.1772
www.mattsoncreative.com

maximo, inc.
United States
619.269.0063
www.maximoinc.com

Maycreate
United States
423.634.0123
www.maycreate.com

McAndrew Kaps
United States
480.580.5113
www.macandrewkaps.com

mccoycreative
United States
360.920.5260
www.mccoycreative.com

McGuire Design
United States
210.884.4609
www.mcguiredesign.com

McMillian Design
United States
718.636.2097
www.mcmilliandesign.com

MEME ENGINE
United States
212.203.5787
www.memeengine.com

Methodologie
United States
206.623.1044
www.methodologie.com

Metroparks of the Toledo Area
United States
419.407.9735
www.metroparkstoledo.com

Mez Design
United States
715.331.4523
www.mezdesign.com

Miaso Design
United States
773.575.3776
www.miasodesign.com

Michael Courtney Design, Inc.
United States
206.329.8488
www.michaelcourtneydesign.com

Michael Osborne Design
United States
415.255.0125
www.modsf.com

Miles Design
United States
317.915.8693
www.milesdesign.com

Mindgruve
United States
619.757.1325
www.mindgruve.com

Mindspace
United States
480.221.5817
www.mindspaceonline.com

Mindspike Design, LLC
United States
414.765.2344
www.mindspikedesign.com

MINE
United States
415.647.6463
www.minesf.com

Mires/Ball
United States
619.234.6631
www.miresball.com

Miriello Grafico, Inc.
United States
619.234.1124
www.miriellografico.com

Mirko Ilić Corp
United States
212.481.9737
www.mirkoilic.com

Misenheimer Creative, Inc.
United States
770.667.9355
www.misenheimer.com

mixdesign
United States
219.322.7190
www.mixedupworld.com

Mode Design Studio
United States
214.827.4700
www.modedesignstudio.com

Modern Dog Design Co.
United States
206.789.7667
www.moderndog.com

Mohouse Design Co.
United States
214.321.3193
www.mohousedesign.com

monster design
United States
425.828.7853
www.monsterinvasion.com

Monster Design Company
United States
707.208.5481
www.monsterdesignco.com

Moonsire Design
United States
843.667.3407

Morgan/Mohon
United States
830.990.2888
www.morganmohon.com

morrow mckenzie design
United States
503.222.0331
www.morrowmckenzie.com

Morse and Company Advertising Communication
United States
219.879.1223
www.morseandcompany.com

Moscato Design
United States
630.493.0518

Motorcycle Safety Foundation
United States
949.727.3227
www.msf-usa.org

Motterdesign
Austria
43.5572.3847.0777
www.motter.at

Napoleon design
Brazil
55.11.9935.0300
www.napoleondesign.net

Naughtyfish
Australia
612.9327.7942
www.naughtyfish.com

NeoGine Communication Design Ltd
New Zealand
644.385.1792
www.neogine.co.nz

nicelogo.com
United States
949.677.7324
www.nicelogo.com

Nick Glenn Design
United States
281.814.7976
www.nickglenndesign.com

Nita B. Creative
United States
651.644.2889
www.nitabcreative.com

Noble and associates
United States
417.875.5000
www.noble.net

northfound
United States
215.232.6420
www.northfound.com

Novasoul
United States
818.753.4175
www.novasoul.com

O!
Iceland
354.562.3300
www.oid.is

o2 ideas
United States
205.949.9494
www.o2ideas.com

oakley design studios
United States
503.241.3705
www.oakleydesign.com

Octane
United States
775.323.7887
www.octanestudios.com

octane inc.
United States
828.693.6699
www.hi-testdesign.com

Octavo Designs
United States
301.695.8885
www.8vodesigns.com

ODM oficina de diseño y marketing
Spain
34.956.265.326
www.odmoficina.com

Off-Leash Studios
United States
617.821.5158
www.offleashstudios.com

Olson + Company
United States
612.215.9800
www.oco.com

OmniStudio Inc
United States
202.464.3050
www.omnistudio.com

Onoma, LLC
United States
212.253.6570
www.onomadesign.com

Orange Creative
New Zealand
09.273.3688
www.orangecreative.co.nz

Owen Design
United States
515.244.1515
www.chadowendesign.com

Oxide Design Co.
United States
402.344.0168
www.oxidedesign.com

Parachute Design
United States
612.359.4387
www.parachutedesign.com

Paragon Design International
United States
312.832.1030
www.paragondesigninternational.com

pat sinclair design
United States
610.896.8616
www.patsinclairdesign.com

Paul Black Design
United States
214.537.9780
www.paulblackdesign.com

Peak Seven Advertising
United States
954.574.0810
www.peakseven.com

Pennebaker
United States
713.963.8607
www.pennebaker.com

Perfect Circle Media Group
United States
972.788.0678
www.perfect360.com

Peters Design
United States
720.348.1053
www.karlpeters.com

Peterson & Company
United States
214.954.0522
www.peterson.com

Phillips Design
United States
813.253.2523
www.portfolios.com/phillipsdesign

Pix Design, Inc.
United States
212.563.5701
www.pixdesign.com

Pixel Basement
United States
561.376.1899
www.pixelbasement.com

Pixelspace
United States
828.994.2212
www.pixelspace.com

Pixelube
United States
206.216.0278
www.pixelube.com

Playoff Corporation
United States
817.983.0142

pleitezgallo:: design haus
United States
951.961.1524
www.pleitezgallo.com

Polemic Design
United States
201.978.5677
www.polemicdesign.com

Polkadot
Australia
1.300.139.398
www.polkadot.com.au

PosterV.Design Studio
Denmark
45.45.85.3575
www.pocs-posters.hv

PowerGroove Creative
United States
720.529.0143

Praxis Studios
United States
919.838.1138
www.praxisstudios.com

Project center
United States
770.979.7684
www.balkecreative.com

Propeller Design
United Arab Emirates
971.4391.4849
www.propeller.ae

proteus
United States
617.263.2211
www.proteusdesign.com

Q
Germany
49.611.181310
www.q-home.de

Quest Fore
United States
412.381.6670
www.questfore.com

R&D Thinktank
United States
214.515.9851
www.randdthinktank.com

R&R Partners
United States
702.318.4360
www.rrpartners.com

rajasandhu.com
Canada
647.668.2547
www.rajasandhu.com

Ramp
United States
213.617.1445
www.rampcreative.com

Red Circle Agency
United States
612.372.4612
www.redcircleagency.com

reduced fat
United States
518.533.9621
www.reduced-fat.com

rehab* communication graphics
United States
206.794.4209
www.rehabgraphics.com

REINES DESIGN INC.
United States
305.373.3181
www.reinesdesign.com

retropup
United States
973.723.5420
www.retropup.com

Reynolds + Associates
United States
310.698.9330
www.372interactive.com

Richards Brock Miller Mitchell & Associates /RBMM
United States
214.987.6500
www.rbmm.com

Rick Johnson & Company
United States
505.266.1100
www.rjc.com

Rickabaugh Graphics
United States
614.337.2229
www.rickbaughgraphics.com

RIGGS
United States
803.799.5972
www.riggspeak.com

ROAD design inc.
United States
949.494.8020
www.roaddzn.com

ROBOT
United States
210.476.8801
www.robotcreative.com

Robot Agency Studios
United States
832.859.0650
www.robotagency.com

Roger Christian & Co
United States
210.829.1953
www.warmsprings.org

Rome & Gold Creative
United States
505.897.0870
www.rgcreative.com

Ross Creative + Strategy
United States
309.637.7677
www.rosscps.com

Ross Hogin Design
United States
206.443.3930
www.hogin.com

Rotor Design
United States
763.706.3906
www.rotordesign.net

Rule29
United States
630.262.1009
www.rule29.com

Ryan Cooper
United States
303.917.9911

S Design, Inc.
United States
405.608.0556
www.sdesigninc.com

S4LE.com
Canada
905.467.7139
www.s4le.com

Sabet Branding
United States
949.705.9960
www.sabet.com

Sabingrafik, Inc.
United States
760.431.0439
www.tracy.sabin.com

Sakkal Design
United States
425.483.8830
www.sakkal.com

Sam's Garage
United States
720.320.7220
www.samsgarageonline.com

Sandstrom Design
United States
503.248.9466
www.sandstromdesign.com

sarah watson design
United States
206.545.8682
www.sarahwatsondesign.com

Savage Design Group
United States
713.522.1555
www.savagedesign.com

Savage Synapses Unltd.
United States
443.756.4674
www.flotsandjets.com

Sayles Graphic Design, Inc.
United States
515.279.2922
www.saylesdesign.com

Schuster Design Group
United States
214.632.3328

Scott Oeschger Design
United States
610.497.1101
www.scottoeschger.com

SD Graphic Design
United States
617.523.5144
www.delaneygroup.com

Seed Studios
United States
817.431.1405
www.seedstudios.com

Sergio Bianco
Italy
39.185.77.2289
www.sergiobianco.it

Sharp Communications, Inc.
United States
212.892.0002
www.sharpthink.com

sharp pixel
United States
206.226.1030
www.sharppixel.com

Shawn Hazen Graphic Design
United States
510.594.9271
www.shawnhazen.com

sheean design
United States
707.224.5206
www.sheeandesign.com

Shelley Design + Marketing
United States
410.523.2796
www.shelleyllc.com

Shift design
Portugal
351.21.410.5912
www.shiftdesign.pt

Sibley/ Peteet Design
United States
512.473.2333
www.spdaustin.com

silvercreativegroup
United States
203.855.7705
www.silvercreativegroup.com

Simon & Goetz Design
Germany
49.69.96.88.55.0
www.simongoetz.de

Sire Advertising
United States
570.743.3900
www.sireadvertising.com

SKOOTA
United States
919.824.6487
www.skoota.com

Sockeye Creative
United States
503.226.3843
www.sockeyecreative.com

Soho Joe
United States
612.588.8740
www.sohojoe.com

Solo Multimedia, Inc.
United States
785.841.5500
www.solomultimedia.com

Sommese Design
United States
814.353.1951

soupgraphix
United States
619.749.SOUP
www.soupgraphix.com

Special Modern Design
United States
323.258.1212
www.specialmoderndesign.com

Squires & Company
United States
214.939.9194
www.squirescompany.com

Stacy Bormett Design, LLC
United States
651.748.0872

Stand Advertising
United States
716.210.1065
www.standadvertising.com

Starlight Studio
United States
718.302.5600

Stephan and Herr
United States
717.426.2939
www.stephanherr.com

Sterling Brands
United States
212.329.4600
www.sterlingbrands.com

Steven O'Connor
United States
323.779.5600

Steve's Portfolio
United States
215.840.0880
www.stevesportfolio.net

Stiles + co
United States
503.806.4670
www.stilesandco.com

Stiles Design
United States
512.443.2102

Stoltze Design
United States
617.350.7109
www.stoltze.com

Straka Dusan/Straka Design
Germany
49.179.126.8229
www.hofd.net

Strange Ideas
United States
316.259.4374

Strategic America
United States
515.453.2000
www.strategicamerica.com

Strategy Studio
United States
212.966.7800
www.strategy-studio.com

strategyone
United States
630.790.9050
www.strategyone.com

stressdesign
United States
315.422.3231
www.stressdesign.com

Studio Arts and Letters
United States
303.298.9911
www.studioartsandletters.com

Studio D
United States
212.563.5600
www.studiodny.com

Studio GT&P
Italy
39.074.232.0372
www.tobanelli.it

Studio Simon
United States
502.479.8447
www.studiosimon.net

Studio Stubborn Sideburn
United States
206.709.8970
www.stubbornsideburn.com

STUN Design and Advertising
United States
225.381.7266
www.stundesign.net

Stuph Clothing
United States
800.242.9166
www.uthstuph.com

Suburban Utopia
United States
706.425.8836
www.suburbanutopia.com

SUMO
United Kingdom
0191.261.9894
www.sumodesign.co.uk

Sutter Design
United States
301.459.5445
www.sutterdesign.com

switchfoot creative
United States
760.720.4255
www.switchfootcreative.com

Synergy Graphix
United States
212.968.7568
www.synergygraphix.com

Tactical Magic
United States
901.722.3001
www.tacticalmagic.com

Tactix Creative
United States
480.225.1480
www.tactixcreative.com

Tallgrass Studios
United States
785.887.6049
www.tallgrassstudios.com

tanagram partners
United States
312.876.3668
www.tanagram.com

TBF Creative
United States
602.722.7995
www.tbfcreative.com

Tchopshop Media
United States
504.895.0000
www.tchopshop.com

tesser inc.
United States
415.541.9999
www.tesser.com

the atmosfear
United States
702.355.8896
www.theatmosfear.com

The Clockwork Group
United States
210.798.1000
www.theclockworkgroup.com

The Collaboration
United States
913.271.3603
www.the-collaboration.com

The Design Poole
United States
206.301.9282
www.thedesignpoole.com

The Envision Group
United States
303.843.9777
www.envision-grp.com

The Flores Shop
United States
804.304.6731
www.thefloresshop.com

The Gate Worldwide
United States
212.508.3400
www.thegateworldwide.com

The Joe Bosack Graphic Design Co.
United States
215.766.1461
www.joebosack.com

The Logo Factory Inc.
Canada
905.564.6747
www.thelogofactory.com

The Meyocks Group
United States
515.225.1200
www.outofthebox.com

The Oesterle
Germany
00.49.89.130.178.74
www.the-oesterle.com

The Pink Pear Design Company
United States
816.519.7327
www.pinkpear.com

The Robin Shepherd Group
United States
904.359.0981
www.trsg.net

The zen kitchen
United States
401.787.5178
www.daniordin.net

thehappycorp global
United States
646.613.1220
www.thehappycorp.com

Thielen Designs
United States
505.396.3900
www.ThielenDesigns.com

Think Tank Creative
United States
337.989.4018

Thomas Manss & Company
United Kingdom
44.20.7251.7777
www.manss.com

thomas-vasquez.com
United States
718.422.1948

Tiffany Design
United States
714.467.8428

Tim Frame Design
United States
937.766.3749
www.timframe.com

Times Infinity
United States
713.224.6200
www.times-infinity.com

Timpano Group
United States
608.251.0808
www.timpanogroup.com

Todd M. LeMieux
United States
413.747.9321
www.toddlemieux.com

Tom Fowler, Inc.
United States
203.845.0700
www.tomfowlerinc.com

traci jones design
United States
303.447.8202
www.commarts-boulder.com

Tribe Design
United States
713.523.5119
www.tribedesign.com

Tungld Advertising Agency
Iceland
354.533.2323
www.tungl.is

Turner Duckworth
United States / United Kingdom
415.675.7777 / 44.0.20.8994.7190
www.TurnerDuckworth.com

Turney Creative
United States
858.349.6370
www.turneycreative.com

Type G
United States
858.792.7333
www.typegdesign.com

Typonic
United Kingdom
44.13.7655.4823
www.typonic.com

Uhlein Design
United States
215.206.2733
www.uhleindesign.com

UlrichPinciotti Design Group
United States
419.255.4515
www.updesigngroup.com

UltraVirgo Creative
United States
646.638.0813
www.ultravirgo.com

Unibrand Belgrade
Turkmenistan
993.81.11.3285.257
www.unibrand360.com

Univisual
Italy
39.02.668.4268
www.univisual.it

UNO
United States
612.874.1920
www.unoonline.com

urbanINFLUENCE design studio
United States
206.219.3599
www.urbaninfluence.com

V V N Design
United States
706.903.2410
www.vvndesign.com

Velocity Design Works
Canada
204.475.0514
www.velocitydesignworks.com

Vigor Graphic Design, LLC.
United States
717.234.4846
www.vigorgraphics.net

Vincent Burkhead Studio
United States
619.787.9384
www.VincentBurkhead.com

Visual Coolness
United States
520.722.6364
www.visualcoolness.com

Visual Inventor Ltd. Co.
United States
405.842.6768
www.VisualInventor.com

Visual Moxie
United States
805.277.4741
www.visualmoxie.com

VMA
United States
937.233.7500
www.vmai.com

Wallace Church, Inc.
United States
212.755.2903
www.wallacechurch.com

Walsh Associates
United States
918.743.9600
www.walshassoc.com

Wells Fargo Financial
United States
515.557.7825

Werner Design Werks
United States
612.338.2550
www.wdw.com

Weylon Smith
United States
615.306.1485

Whaley Design, Ltd
United States
651.645.3463
www.whaleydesign.com

Whence: the studio
United States
504.338.2994
www.michaelnixdesign.com

Whitney Edwards LLC
United States
410.822.8335
www.wedesign.com

Wholesale Distributors
United States
206.290.7017
www.wd-usa.com

Who's the Min/ Creative Solutions
United States
973.219.2335
www.whosthemin.com

Wilkinson Media, Inc.
United States
609.818.0363
www.wilkinsonmedia.net

Willoughby Design Group
United States
816.561.4189
www.willoughbydesign.com

Wolken communica
United States
206.545.1696
www.wolkencommunica.com

Wray Ward Laseter
United States
704.332.9071
www.wwlcreative.com

www.iseedots.com
United States
619.955.8178
www.iseedots.com

Yellobee Studio
United States
404.249.6407
www.yellobee.com

Yellow Fin Studio
United States
512.472.3227
www.yellowfinstudio.com

Yellow Pencil Brand Sharpening
New Zealand
64.365.0080
www.yellowpencil.co.nz

ykcreative, LLC
United States
832.752.6402
www.ykcreative.com

Zapata Design
United States
281.785.0242
www.zapatadesign.com

ZEBRA design branding
Russia
7.8482.485684

Zed + Zed + Eye Creative Communications
United States
352.572.3474
www.zedzedeye.com

zengigi design
United States
301.562.9406
www.zengigi.com

Zipper Design
United States
206.818.9101
www.zipperd.com

Zombie Design
United States
801.299.1567
www.designzombie.com

ZONA Design
United States
212.244.2900
www.zonadesign.com

Zwölf Sonnen Design
Germany
49.06.114.504.942
www.zwoelfsonnen.de

about the authors

Bill Gardner is president of Gardner Design and has produced work for Bombardier/Learjet, Thermos, Nissan, Pepsi, Pizza Hut, Coleman Outdoor, Excel, Cargill Corporation, and the 2004 Athens Olympics. His work has been featured in *Communication Arts, Print, Graphis, New York Art Directors, STEP inside design,* Mead Top 60, the Museum of Modern Art, and many other national and international design exhibitions. His works and writings about corporate identity and three-dimensional design have been published in numerous books and periodicals. Gardner has judged a number of national and international design competitions, including the *Communication Arts Design Annual.*

He is the founding president of the American Institute of Graphic Arts, Wichita Chapter, where he continues to serve on the board of directors. Gardner also serves on the AIGA Chapter Development Guidelines Committee, the Kansas State University Design Advisory Panel, and the Wichita State University Design Faculty Selection Committee. In addition, he was the founding director of the Kansas Student Portfolio Scholarship Forum and a coordinator of the AIGA Midwest Chapter Retreat.

Catharine Fishel is a freelance writer and editor who specializes in graphic design. She is the author of many books on the subject; contributes to many magazines, including *PRINT* and *Communication Arts;* and is editor of LogoLounge.com.